Fred Panton

Man on a Mission

Whether:

Building a very successful poultry business,

Acquiring a wonderful wife,

Tracing the wartime grave of his brother Chris,

Searching for the Canadian pilot who flew Chris's plane,

Buying and restoring a Lancaster bomber,

Or establishing The Aviation Heritage Centre as a memorial to all the bomber crews lost in WWII –

Fred Panton has always been a

Man on a Mission

**Written by Kate Panton, as told to her
by her grandfather, Fred Panton**

Propagator Press

This book is published by Propagator Press

Propagator Press
38 Parkside Road
Leeds
LS6 4NB

ISBN   978-1-908037-20-6   Paperback

Designed by Propagator Press
Printed in Great Britain

Foreword

As one of my Grandfather's eight grandchildren, I feel very privileged to have been the one to write his book, as I am sure that all my cousins would have done him great justice.

Since we were children, he has told us enthralling stories of his adventures in life, which he always manages to tell in exactly the same words every single time. All eight of us have encouraged him to put his exciting adventures into a book so that they can live on and also as a full explanation of the birth of his Aviation Heritage Centre, home of his beloved Lancaster bomber, "Just Jane".

During our time together writing this book, Grandad's stories have brought me tears of both laughter and sadness and have stirred every emotion, which we both hope you will also feel as you make your way through his adventures.

This book is written in the same way that he tells his stories; down to earth, honest, totally captivating and with his unique storytelling style and local colloquialisms.

It's been a very special journey writing this book with Grandad. I've really appreciated all the time spent working with him over the last three years, and it has given me wonderful memories which I shall cherish forever.

Kate Panton

Fred and Kate at Durnbach War Cemetery

Contents

Chapter One

Moving around

Finding (and thawing) our feet!

I'm going to start by taking you back to the very beginning, to the day that I was born, on the 6th of March 1931, in a place called Asgarby, near Spilsby, in Lincolnshire. My father, Edward Stoat Panton, was a shepherd on Mr Walter Dunham's farm. Now, it was lambing season when I was born, so in order to look after both the sheep and my mother, Amy Panton, he kept all the sheep and lambs gathered outside the house so that he didn't have too far to walk to look after my Mother…or the sheep! We were having a particularly bad winter, with twelve to fourteen inches of snow on the ground for quite a while. This meant that my parents were unable to get out of the farm to get me registered, as we were quite a distance from the town, so my birth went unrecorded at this point. It wasn't until I needed a passport in 1971, that I found out that I wasn't registered and it appeared that it was going to be quite difficult to prove that I was English. I was only able to get one thanks to a lady called Mrs Pinning from a little village called Lusby, which joined onto Asgarby and which was only a mile and a half away from where I was born. Mrs Pinning was a Sunday school teacher, so she used to teach my elder brothers and sisters and she was also very good friends with my mother and father. She remembered my birth, so was able to give the necessary proof and that was the only way that I was able to get my certificate registered. It was a bit worrying at the time, and very lucky she was still alive and that she remembered it well.

Shortly after I was born, my Father decided to leave Asgarby farm, moving not too far to a village called Ashby. We moved on April 6th 1931, which was the date known as "Lady day" or "Flitting day", which, in the agricultural world, was the one day of the year, back in those days, when you could move from one farm to another. I was only four weeks old when we moved to Ashby and at this point I had four elder sisters; Bessie, Evelyn, Gwen and Freda. I also had two elder brothers, Roland and Christopher, making me the seventh child.

According to my father, when we moved the seven miles from Asgarby to Ashby, we went by horse and wagon and managed to move all of our furniture and belongings, as well as the nine of us, on this one wagon. Now, the previous occupants of the farm at Ashby were expected to be vacated from the house by the time we turned up, but to my parents' surprise, on our arrival at half past seven in the morning, we found them in the kitchen, still having their breakfasts! So we had to wait outside until they had finished before we could move in! It was normal for families of this type to move so early in the morning, because wagoners normally start work between five and six o'clock in the morning, so although this may seem very early today, it was very common back in those days.

My father worked as a stockman and wagoner on this farm for Mr English and we stayed here for three years. My father decided to move again, on 6th April 1934, to a place called Skendleby Holmes, in Partney, Lincolnshire. He began by working on farms again, until Butlin's Holiday camp began being built, in Skegness, where they were recruiting men to work as navvies. My Father decided to take one of these jobs helping to build the holiday camp, for an extra one shilling per day (the equivalent of five pence in new money.) This meant he had to cycle from Partney to Skegness, which is fourteen miles; a twenty eight mile round journey every day. In those days, for my father, a full week's wage worked out at around One pound, ten shillings and ten pence. (£1.55 in new money.) To help this make sense in monetary value of today, if you were earning one pound and twelve shillings per week in the mid-1930s, then compared to today, over seventy years later, the equivalent wage would be £200 - £250 per week.

Previous to this, back in 1933, I had a little brother arrive and he was named Harold, which made our family eight children; four girls and four boys. Of course, even in those days you would say that my father was very, very poor and, as I became older, my father told me that when we were all young, there wasn't a week passed that one of us didn't need a pair of new boots or shoes! And I often think back, what a hard life my father and mother had bringing us all up. My father had been in the First World War and came away wounded and I do realise now, how hard they had to work to keep us.

I would just like to say a few words here about my mother and I really cannot speak highly enough of her. She was a very small, petite lady, even though she'd had eight children. She didn't have washing machines or any modern electrical things that we have today; she only had washtubs and mangles, paraffin lamps, etc. She worked so hard and she absolutely lived for her children; you couldn't get a better mother, she would give her last crumb away. One thing I remember very well about her is that she had beautiful long, brown hair, which came down to her waist and you know, it never started to go grey until she was in her nineties. One of my fondest childhood memories of her is that on a Sunday evening, she would sit in a chair by the fire and just comb her hair for hours and I would sit with her and watch her combing. I really remember that very well. She was a very slim lady and she never took tablets for the whole of her life. If she had a headache she would just bathe her head with water and the only time that she ever took any was after my father died and the Doctor gave her something to help her cope with it, but she only took two tablets and then wouldn't have any more. She lived to be ninety five years old. I couldn't have wished for a better mother and I still don't know how she managed to get all her work done and to raise us all and to keep her home so well. I know that my brothers and sisters would agree with every word that I've said about her. There's one thing that I noticed from a very young age, in fact, all the time I lived at home and worked with Mother and Father. Every time he came in and out of the house, to and from work, coming in and out for meals, my father would always give my mother a kiss and he never missed, he always stopped to give her a kiss; and because of that I've carried on the tradition with my wife.

In 1936, when I was five years old I started school at Partney. I shall always remember when I started school because we, my brothers, sisters and I had to walk across three fields to travel from where we lived to the village school. In those days, we used to get very harsh frosts and snow. We would wear boots everyday and the boots that I had to go to school in, had a hole in the bottom of each foot. So on really frosty, hard mornings before we went to school, Mother would put cardboard at the bottom of our boots to fill the holes, hoping that the frost wouldn't come through. But before I would even get near school, while walking through the fields, the cardboard in my boots would become wet and rotten, which meant I had to walk on the sides of my feet for the rest of the journey to stop them from getting cold!
I always remembered that very well.

When I started school at Partney, I came to enjoy my time there very much and this is because I had a very nice teacher. We called her Miss Mastin. She really did look after me and I grew to think a lot of her. And as it turned out, years later, when I got married, I found out that my teacher at Partney was my wife's aunt.

Not many years later, my father decided to leave again and we went to live in the small town of Spilsby, in a place called Queen's Street, Wellington Yard. I started another school and my teacher there, Miss Smith, was very good to me. I have a story that my grandchildren particularly enjoy about my time living in Spilsby as a small boy. I would have been about eight or nine years of age, somewhere between 1936 and 1939 on Guy Fawkes night. My brother, Roly, had bought this rocket. It was a very big one for those days, because it stood around three feet high. It was certainly the biggest rocket I had ever seen. That night, Roly stood the rocket upright in a jar, lit it and let it off into the sky, and you know, it was the best rocket I had ever seen. It went very high and it was very bright in the dark sky, it was wonderful. After seeing that, I thought to myself, "I'm going to buy one of those next year," but I knew that I would have to start saving my pennies up to buy such a big one like brother Roland's!

In Spilsby, there was a small shop that sold fishing tackle, toys and all manner of things like that, including fireworks when it got close to Guy Fawkes Night each year. So I started taking my pennies to this shop and they would save them until I had enough to buy the big rocket that I wanted. I can't remember how much it cost, but it was such a big rocket. There was this gentleman who also lived in Wellington Yard called Mr Briggs, who was a market gardener and whenever he saw me in Spilsby, even if I was on the other side of the road, he would always put his hand in his pocket and throw me a penny so that I could take it to the little shop to help pay for my rocket. I remember that my mother sold her sewing machine to someone who used to come round, because she didn't need it anymore. He gave her a penny for it, which she gave to me and I took it straight across to the shop for my rocket fund! Finally, Guy Fawkes Night came round again and I'd just finished paying for 'my' rocket, so I rushed to the shop to collect it. Now, I'd never told any of my family about buying this rocket and when it was really dark that night, I took my rocket outside and stood it in a jar, just like I'd watched Roly do the year before. I got my box of matches and lit this big rocket that I'd spent all year saving for and as I lit it, the sparks flew all about the place. The next thing that happened was that the rocket went sideways in the jar and flew straight through Brigg's window, the man who had given me most of the money to buy this rocket! It was a Friday night and he was sitting in his armchair reading his newspaper when this rocket shot straight through his window, through the middle of the paper he was reading and just missed his head. It hit the wall on the other side to where he was sitting and the stick landed on the sideboard in the house! So after watching my rocket fly into his window, I bolted into the house and hid under the table, which had this big green tablecloth that nearly went down to the floor. So I sat under the table, behind the safety of the long tablecloth with my legs crossed, shaking with fear! A few minutes later I heard some footsteps coming down the path and a knock on the door. Father went to open it to find Mrs Briggs there, and she said to my father, "Has one of your boys let a rocket off Mr Panton?" and my father said to her, "I wouldn't be surprised Mrs Briggs, he's sitting under the table," nodding his head towards where I was hiding! "Well," she said, "It's gone straight through our window and it only just missed Briggy's head; it went through the paper he was reading, landed on our sideboard and I've brought the stick for him to play with." We had to pay to have a new pane of glass, which brother Roly paid for; one and four pence. And that's all that was made of it. Evenwhen we came back from Nottinghamshire in the 1940s, I'd never heard another thing about it, until years later, during the 1970s. There was a man who I never even knew existed, but he was a relation of Mr Briggs somehow and he owned the fish and chip shop in Spilsby. I'd never seen him before in my life, but he certainly seemed to know me, because he always said to me, "Here comes the rocket man!"

When we came to Spilsby, my Father was still working in Skegness at Butlins Holiday Camp, cycling everyday still for one shilling extra. At that point, in his spare time, he was taking up rabbit catching and started a role as a part-time gamekeeper, which he enjoyed doing very much. Father worked at Butlins through the whole construction process. He started working there in 1936 and it was completed in late 1939, so it took just under three years to finish. He decided that he would stop working at Butlins once it was completed. He had found a gamekeeping and rabbit catching job advertised in North Nottinghamshire between Worksop and Retford, situated on a large estate of 10,000 acres. He applied for the job and took it, meaning that we would move once again.

I'll give you the story of my father's post interview conversation with Mr Wadds, the head keeper on the Osberton estate. After my father applied for the job, he was called for an interview. The job opening was for two gamekeepers, so my father's friend, Mr Padley, also applied and they went to Osberton together from Spilsby and took a train to Worksop, where they were collected by Mr Wadds. After the interview, they were both accepted for the job and as Mr Wadds was taking them back to the train station at Worksop, he said to them both, "There's just one thing that I forgot to mention to you; if you're afraid to go out at night, then it's no good you coming here. And if anybody should knock on your door after 11 o'clock at night, never put your head out of the window to see who it is. And don't go wandering around on your own at that time of night either." After Mr Wadds told them this, Mr Padley decided that he didn't want to take the job anymore, whereas Father still accepted the job and prepared us for moving. So that gives you an idea of how life used to be back in those days; all the food rationing made gamekeeping a very dangerous job, as people became desperate with starvation and took to poaching to survive.

We moved in 1939, to a place called the Osberton estate, which was owned by a Captain Fuljambe. The day that we moved there, we travelled in the back of a lorry, because we had been fetched by the estate lorry, all the way from Spilsby, which was quite a privilege to have been collected. So we all rode in this lorry. You can imagine my brothers and sisters with our mother in the back, all of us sitting together on our sofa and on our chairs, amongst our other belongings, bumping and shuffling along on the old roads in this lorry, with no modern power-steering. That certainly wasn't sophisticated or comfortable by today's standards! Whilst we were in the back, Father sat in the cab with the driver. It was April, because, as you now know, we moved on flitting day and the weather was really quite pleasant, which was a blessing, because the back of the lorry had open vents, so had it been very cold or raining, then we would have really suffered!

By this time, I was eight years of age and my brothers and sisters went to school on the estate, in a village called Scofton. Just to give you an idea of what my father did, it varied for each place that he worked. On some farms he was a wagoner with horses, sometimes he worked as a shepherd, or at other times, he was employed as an ordinary agricultural worker in the fields. All farm labourers seemed to move around quite a lot back in those days and one of the main reasons that my father would move on, is because he would have been offered more money from another farm employer, which he would obviously take due to the size of his family. Looking back to all the times that we moved, maybe an average of nearly every three years, I very much view it as having been very educational.

I am sure that I can say with absolute certainty that Osberton was one of the loveliest and most beautiful places that I have ever lived. I would also like to point out at this stage that Father was a local Methodist lay preacher and I really did think a lot of my father and mother. Now, my father's father had been a lay preacher and then my father became a lay preacher, which meant that we were all brought up in a Christian home. When my father died, he had been preaching for just over fifty years. He took up his preaching when he came out of his army service after the First World War and he had a certificate to show that he had been a preacher for over fifty years. In those days nobody ever worked on farms on Sundays and this is how he was able to find time to do his preaching as well as working full time and supporting his family. To continue our family tradition, my younger brother, Harold, took after my father, as he started to take up local preaching in the sixties and he still does it to this day. So with our Methodist upbringing, we were all brought up to be very active within the Church and the lessons from my upbringing have stayed with me all through my life and have been carried into every aspect of my life, including my family and my business. I was brought up and taught from my very early years to treat everybody the same as you would want to be treated yourself, which means that when I do deals now, I make sure that the other people involved are all happy. I always try to be straight and honest, then there are never any problems in the future; it can never come back against you. Always be straight and honest, that's always been my principle and it will pay dividends in the end.

Back to my childhood; every Saturday, even at the age of eight, I always went with my father, keepering or rabbit catching. He would take me with him on his bicycle, sitting on the cross bar as we rode through the estate to different parts, admiring all the beautiful woods and the rhododendrons. We lived at a place called Rayton Angles on the estate, in a cottage that was split into three. Our family lived at one end, and Jim Blakey, who was also a game keeper, with his wife and son in the middle and on the far end, was a Mr Riley, who worked on one of the tenant farms on the estate. Our cottage was on the side of a very large wood, which was named Scofton wood and it must have been almost one mile square. We used to have to walk right through the middle of this wood to get to Scofton village, where we went to school each morning. In the spring and summer time, as we travelled through the woods, we'd see the pheasants walking and running around; it was a sight that nobody could ever forget. Then when autumn arrived, all the trees would change colours and the leaves would start falling from the branches, creating a brown and golden thick, leafy carpet, which we enjoyed walking through. The smell of autumn; all the oak, ash, fir and beech trees in this wood created a fantastic smell and coming home from school, around 4 o'clock at night, walking through this scenery that was so pretty, left a permanent impression on me that I will never forget. It really was a lovely place to live. In fact my mother never wanted to leave. It was the one place that she really loved and wanted to stay, it was so peaceful, nice and quiet and we all loved living there.

Farm workers and land army girls relax in the snow at Osberton

Chapter Two

Break out of the War

A shaky start to gamekeeping!

Back in 1939, the Second World War broke out and I shall always remember the day war was announced, because the following day, I daren't get up out of bed for fear the Germans would be here. As I recall, it was near 12 o'clock before I summoned the bravery to get up! The announcement was to start a complete new era in our way of thinking and working. I remember the very first night that the Germans came to bomb Sheffield. Rayton Angles was only sixteen miles across country to Sheffield and from where we lived and we could see the enormous barrage balloons around the city being used to try and stop the Nazi planes from coming over. That first night, the bombing started at 9 o'clock and carried on continuously through the night until 5 o'clock the next morning. The windows and doors of our house never stopped chipping and napping from the vibrations of the bombs being dropped sixteen miles away. After the first night of bombing over Sheffield, there was another bombing raid almost every week. Ten to fifteen minutes before the bombing began, sirens would go off in the Manton coal mine, to warn us all when the next raid was on the way to the city. But as time went on, gradually we knew there was going to be a raid before the sirens even started, because all the pheasants in the wood would start calling out and become uneasy. They would know at least twenty minutes before the sirens, so we realised there would be another raid that night.

My brother, Christopher, who was seven years older than me, had decided to join the Air Training Corp at Worksop. Chris, of course, had left school and was training as a gamekeeper on the Osberton estate up until then. So this made the beginning of the war a particularly worrying and frightening time for my parents. As the war went on and the bombing raids became more incessant, my father decided he would build an air raid shelter for us all. So he dug this shelter in the wood and it was quite a large thing to dig using only a spade. He lined it with planks of wood that the estate had given him from the wood yard and he made it so that we were able to sit around together safely in a circle. He covered it with strong metal, then again in soil to camouflage it and he made good strong steps for us to climb

9

down into the shelter. The Germans came to bomb Sheffield again soon after and we all made our way into the shelter that Father had created for us, with his own two hands, to keep us safe. There would be my young brother Harold, Christopher, my two youngest sisters, my father, mother and myself. My brother and sisters who weren't living with us at that stage included my second eldest sister, Evelyn, who was away for service in the WAAFs, stationed at North Weald, the Essex airfield from which many of the Battle of Britain Spitfires were flown. My eldest brother, Roland, was back in Lincolnshire working on a dairy farm for the Dennett family, as was my eldest sister Bessie. So this left the rest of us; Harold, Gwen, Freda, Chris and me at Osberton. What I remember most vividly about this air raid shelter, was that, although we were as much as sixteen miles away, the vibrations caused from the bombs dropping would make the sand in the ground creep down through the joints in the metal cover and it would come in and trickle down your back. This would make us even more nervous and frightened, so as you can imagine, it was quite an experience to live through.

In 1940, when I was nine years of age, I started to become very interested in chickens and poultry. I had around twenty chickens in a hut, which I would clean out and look after every Saturday and I would have it all cleaned out before 7 o'clock in the morning, so that I would still be able to go with my father through the wood, rabbit catching. There were food shortages and rationing at the time, so keeping hens and catching rabbits were good ways of making sure that our family always had meat and eggs available. Then, in 1941 at the age of ten, with my young experience of keeping chickens, I got a little paid job, working on the dairy farm on the estate, where there was a herd of quite a special type of Jersey cow. It was a very up-to-date dairy farm in those days and I would work there on Saturdays, Sundays and holiday time up until we left Osberton. I always remember when we came back to Lincolnshire. On my last day working there, the head herdsman on the estate, a Mr Miller, presented me with an envelope to give to my parents. As it turned out, Mr Miller had rewarded me with a brand new pound note and a reference, but somehow or other we managed to keep the pound note, but lost the reference! I didn't quite understand the gravity of the meaning of a generous reference at the time!

During my school days in Osberton, I particularly enjoyed the autumn and winter time. In the two classrooms of our school we used to have two quite large stoves which had flat, round rings around each one, heated by coal. The teachers would allow all the children in each of the classes to take potatoes in the morning and place each one side by side, all along the stove rings, and they would roast there all morning until lunch time. I can still taste how beautiful those potatoes were, being roasted like that all morning.

Every Saturday morning, my father would travel to Worksop to do the shopping for Mother and he would always return with a large piece of slab cake for us all. My brothers and sisters would each take a piece of this cake to school after the weekend. So I would always look forward to Monday mornings when I would enjoy this cake, which, during the war days was a real luxury. This is something that has always stood out in my memory. Another thing which I do remember very well; at playtime which would be between ten and eleven in the morning, we would see all the different gamekeepers arriving on their bikes, coming to hang all their rabbits in the Head Keeper's larder and I always enjoyed watching this. In those days, all the pleasure gardens, as they used to be called at Osberton Hall, had keepers who would wear green overalls in the summer and brown overalls in the wintertime. This was to keep them as camouflaged as possible to poachers and wildlife for each respective season. Seeing the keepers at Osberton and going rabbit catching with Father started the development of my own keen interest; it really was a magical place to live. My passion for keepering has been in my blood, if you like.

I remember that Chris used to be very good at drawing. He was very artistic and he particularly liked things to do with the Navy, like drawing battleships, etc. One Sunday, Chris and I went for a walk around the estate and went to one of the posts where the guns used to stand when they were shooting pheasants. We had brought a big 100 weight hessian bag with us and filled it to overflowing with the empty cartridges that fall to the floor once the gun has been fired. After we had got the bag as full as we could, we walked home and Chris tipped the whole bag out, emptying all the cartridges all over the floor. Then, he filled the room by building a huge model of a battleship, using these empty cartridges that we had collected, standing them up, very close to one another. It really was impressive.

I would like to recall with you, the very first Sunday we moved from Spilsby to Osberton; a humorous little story which my father shared with me a few years later. Our next door neighbour, who was also a game keeper, was called Jim Blakey and, to give you an image of Mr Blakey, he was a huge, intimidating tower of a man who stood over 6 feet tall and weighed more than eighteen stone. You can imagine how a man of this stature, with the brutal temper that he had, would have looked to my eight year old self! Mr Blakey and my father were a paired team for night duty, as it was much safer for keepers to work in pairs at night time, because of poachers. Anyway, Mr Blakey had just sat down to his Sunday lunch, when two of his friends from Worksop came to see him and informed him of some poachers they had spotted at a place called Carlton forest, which was only four fields distant from Rayton Angles, on the estate. There were two men with two dogs, chasing hares and this was on Blakey's beat, where they should not have been. By this point, Blakey was absolutely outraged at having his roast dinner interrupted. He came round to my father and knocked on our door and said that he wanted him to come and help catch these poachers. So off they went through the fields on their bicycles and they eventually caught them and Father told me that Mr Blakey grabbed hold of the first man by his shoulders and started to shake him like a leaf, "What do you think you're doing chasing my old hares' guts out? What *do* they call you? Where *do* you come from?" he was shouting at him! And the man was so nervous that he started to stutter… unable to say a thing, he kept stuttering and Blakey kept shouting over him, "What *do* they call you? Where *do* you come from?" The poor man kept stuttering and couldn't get a word out, even if he had wanted to! My father, while all this was going on, was standing behind Mr Blakey and Father started to laugh uncontrollably at the sight of this man stuttering and Blakey shouting at him in blind rage, shaking him like he was no heavier than a tea bag. Blakey then turned round to the other poacher and shouted, "What *do* they call him? Where *does* he come from?" And so, the other man started to stutter too and on it went, until eventually, both my father and Blakey did manage to find out what their names were.

On their journey home they had to push their bikes up a hill and walk, due to the sand because it used to be very sandy and dry near Worksop. Getting round the estate could be difficult and on this occasion, the sand made it impossible to ride, so they had to push their bikes up the hill. Blakey always, without fail, took the lead when they were out after poachers at night and so Father was walking behind and was still smiling and laughing to himself, when Mr Blakey just happened to turn around and see my Dad laughing to himself. Blakey put his stick in the air, pointing it at Father and angrily said, "I see you laughing; a fairish mate you're going to be! If I see you laughing again, I'll strike you one with this stick!" and he said, "I'll tell Wadds in the morning what sort of a mate you're going to turn out to be." Wadds was the Head keeper at Osberton estate. Anyway, on the Monday morning, my Dad happened to see Mr Wadds and he said, "Have you seen Jim this morning and did he say what happened yesterday?" Wadds hadn't seen Blakey at this point, so Dad told him, and said, "He even threatened me with his stick when he saw me laughing!" Mr Wadds laughed to himself and said, "Ay, he would do Edward, when he's in one of those moods!"

I'd like to point out at this stage that in those days, especially in the wartime, during the rations when meat was scarce, it was a full time job keeping on top of poachers. In those days, a keeper would earn one pound and ten shillings for catching a poacher during the daytime and three pounds for catching a poacher at night, because it was so much more dangerous in the dark. It was a very formidable occupation, being up at night trying to catch poachers. I'll say here, I always knew when Dad was going out after poachers in the dark and they would usually go out at 11 o'clock at night until 4 o'clock the following morning during the winter months when the pheasants were all in season. I wasn't very old at the time, but I did worry about my father being out at night like that and I used to pray to God every night to look after Father whilst he was on his duties in the dark. I remember one year, they were shooting for twenty two days and twenty two nights, every day, non-stop and all the keepers were up every night after the poachers. Of course, they only had bicycles; there were no cars to speak of, or any form of motor transportation. It was a very basic way of moving around and after a few nights of being up every night, my Father told me that after a day's shooting, all the keepers would go and hang their pheasants at Scofton larder as quickly as possible in the hopes of getting away before Wadds could come out and tell them to be back at night. But Mr Wadds, without fail, always came out just as they were getting onto their bicycles to go home! And he would say, "Be here for eleven, lads!" And it went on like this for twenty two days and twenty two nights. Of course, they did a lot more shooting during the day throughout the season, but this particular period was non-stop.

The keepers would always go out in twos and Father and Jim Blakey would go as a pair together. It was arranged that they would all meet at a certain tree at 4 o'clock in the morning, to check they had all been on duty and Mr Wadds, on a very cold night, would give each of the keepers a little tot of brandy to go home with. Father told me, he remembered, once he'd had his brandy he could feel it reaching to the tips of his toes on a very cold night! Of course, during those days we always had snow, every year around ten to twelve inches at Scofton. The keepers would have to walk around the grounds and feed the pheasants their corn by hand, using a sack, throwing it onto the ground. But to see all the snow hanging on the trees and buildings at the Osberton estate meant you were seeing nature at its very best.

I have another fond memory of my time at Osberton and it's one relating to Mr Wadds. He used to have this beautiful, very strong, long stick, which was made out of apple wood and I still have a photograph of him holding this stick. It had fifty three knots down the stem, a V-shaped handle made from part of a deer's antler and a whistle, which was carved out of horn. It made such an impression on me that I decided to have a replica made of this stick that I remember so well. It was only a few years ago that I was fortunate to find a craftsman to be able to make this replica; also made of apple wood, it has 51 knots down the side and I have the "Just Jane" emblem on the top of my stick. This is the same stick that I'm holding in the photograph on the front cover of this book.

One more incident I'll share with you, which I remember very well, includes Mr Blakey again. It goes back to the very first night that they came to bomb Sheffield. We were all in bed and so were Blakey and his family in his house. When the German planes started to drop their bombs, the house started to shudder, doors and windows rattled continuously. This woke my Father and Jim Blakey simultaneously and Father got up and opened the bedroom window to investigate what was happening. Jim had also opened his window and they both happened to put their heads out the window at exactly the same time and, with his head no more than ten feet away, he bellowed at my father, "What the hell's wrong with you, man?" and Dad said, "It's not me, it's the Jerries bombing." "Oh," Jim said, "It's them Bs is it?"

It would have been around 1941 when all this took place. Then quite a blow came to my Father in 1942. The Ministry decided they were going to build an airfield on the estate. We couldn't believe they were going to do this, because it meant cutting down a large amount of the woodlands in order to build it. So my Father was forced to make a decision to move back to Lincolnshire, because the estate wasn't going to need so many gamekeepers. As I had mentioned earlier, Christopher had joined the ATC at Worksop, which meant that he would continue living on the estate, while the rest of the family moved back to Lincolnshire. Chris lodged on the estate with another employee and at this point he was only sixteen or seventeen. At the same time, he also carried on gamekeeping with the head keeper, as well as his ATC training. Chris had volunteered for aircrew and he had been called up for duty just at the time that we were leaving, which is why he stayed. So we left Osberton to return to Lincolnshire, where my Father was born and bred, in the areas of Louth, Binbrook and Maidenwell. We came to live in a place called Old Bolingbroke, near Spilsby, on top of a hill, which was at the foot of the Lincolnshire Wolds, a place called Highfield farm. Highfield farm was owned (and still is) by the Dennet family and Father came back on the condition that he could gamekeep and rabbit catch during the winter months, and work on the farm during the summer months. This being 1942, I would have been eleven years of age at the time. So whenever possible, weekends, holidays and the like, I would go gamekeeping with my father, which I enjoyed doing very much, keepering was starting to get into my blood.

Fred's Early Years

↑ Fred at school

Fred

Edward and Frances Panton

Chapter Three

The Lancaster Bombers Arrive

A very close fly-by!

Some months after our arrival at Old Bolingbroke, they began building an airfield at East Kirkby, which was just over a mile's distance from us. With living on top of the hill, it gave us prime position of viewing the airfield, to watch it grow and progress and to me, as a lad of eleven, it was very interesting and exciting to see all this work being done. It only took eleven months in total to build and it was completed in August of 1943, but no-one at that time had any idea of the type of aircraft that would be arriving at East Kirkby. Then, one Sunday, at quarter to one in the afternoon, the family had gone into the house to have our Sunday lunch and we had just sat down when we heard the sound of engines and my brothers, sisters and I all ran out of the house to see what it was. We ran to the bottom of the little grass paddock, looking towards the airfield and we saw a Lancaster bomber just arriving. It started to circle the airfield; it was very low and it was coming right towards us on top of the hill, circling the airfield. Two to three minutes later another Lancaster arrived, then after two to three minutes another one came and so on. At that point we hardly knew what a Lancaster was, but there they were; powered by four Merlin, Rolls Royce engines, Lancaster Bombers. We finished with nineteen Lancasters circling the airfield before one ever came to land. They got themselves all nicely spaced out, very low, banking over every now and again to have a good look at this new airfield. I can remember it as if it was yesterday and I know that it's a sight I shall never forget. Those Lancasters did something that day I have never seen a Lancaster do again, from that day to this. Although they were very low, the first one coming towards us on the hill suddenly dropped a bit lower and the one behind it jumped a bit higher, the one behind dropped lower, and then the next one higher, until all nineteen Lancasters were going up and down, banking over the Airfield until they were on top of us over the hill. I am sure what they were doing was putting on a bit of a show for us locals, to let us see what we were going to be in for. Then, they went right out towards Sibsey, Stickney, and all the little villages, before coming into land at East Kirkby. They were known as 57 Squadron and had come from RAF Scampton, which was twenty nine miles away, across country. Upon their

17

arrival they certainly didn't waste anytime either, as on that Monday night we could hear their engines strike up as they went on their first bombing raid from their East Kirkby station.

A few weeks later, another Squadron of Lancasters arrived on the airfield and they were known as 630 Squadron. So we had forty eight Lancasters at East Kirkby in total, twenty four Lancasters on either side and they would stand equally spaced out on the airfield, each squadron on opposite sides, around one hundred to two hundred metres apart. Whenever they took off to go on their bombing raids, it was very, very rare that we missed going to watch them take off. As lads, we might be playing around in Old Bolingbroke until late at night, as we had double summer time then and it stayed light until 11 o'clock at night. So whenever the Lancasters took off, we nearly always managed to go and watch. Usually they would leave around 7 o'clock at night and it didn't matter which direction the wind was blowing, even if it was blowing in the opposite direction to where we lived, we could still hear the Lancaster engines start. So we would say to each other, "The Lancs are going to take off!" and we all ran and biked to get down to the beginning of the runway to watch them take off and that was so exciting for us. We would stand on the main road from Spilsby to East Kirkby and the Lancasters would nearly always come over this main road, from one road to the other. There were three runways, each just slightly over one mile long and the runway nearest the main road was no more than one hundred and twenty metres away.

We would stand watching on the main road at the end of the runway and there would be anything from ten, twenty, thirty, forty, sometimes even fifty people standing on either side of the road to watch them take off. And never once did anyone come over and say to us, "You must stand back, it's dangerous." You could stand anywhere you liked, even in the middle of the road to watch, but we were never warned about the dangers. You see, there weren't so many civilian cars on the roads in those days; if you saw one civilian car in twenty four hours then you'd be doing well, as it was mainly military vehicles. When those Lancasters were taking off, us lads used to like watching to see how long they would take to leave the runway, you see the longer they took taking off, the lower they would be to the ground as they came over head, which we would always enjoy. However, I realise now what a selfish way to think this was, because it was due to the weight of their bombs, ammunition and fuel which would make them struggle to get airborne, when they were at their maximum capacity, it was a very difficult and risky task.

If I had to put a bet with you how high the Lancasters would be off the ground as they flew over head, where we stood, if you said any higher than 50ft, you'd lose your bet! And never once, while we were standing on the road watching, did the pilots or flight engineers ever look or wave at us, standing in the crowd. They would be looking straight ahead, really struggling to get airborne. The mid-upper gunner would occasionally wave to us, and the rear gunner would sometimes move his guns in a wave of acknowledgement. But the pilots would always be looking dead straight ahead, concentrating on getting the plane off the ground.

After a time of watching them taking off, my friend and I, who I sat next to at Bolingbroke school, decided one night, when they were going to be taking off, that we would go and sit in the centre of the road, at the end of the runway, to see what it was like to let a Lancaster fly over the top of our heads. But in order to do this we had to lie down side-by-side, flat on the road because it was too dangerous to stand up. So there we were, lying down at the end of the road and then the Lancaster started to come down the runway to take off. Just as it started to leave the ground and launch overhead, it seemed, for a split second, just to hang there in the air. Of course it didn't, but it felt like a long time underneath and it frightened us. It would take me ten minutes to tell you what some of the people there said to us as we got up after the Lancaster had gone and I couldn't repeat most of it! We certainly never did it again and I'll tell you why. When a Lancaster is going to take off at the end of the runway, with a maximum load of ten tonnes, six tanks full of petrol, seven men and their ammunition, it would be another nineteen tonnes above its body weight, on a runway which is only one mile long; it would have to have reached at least 103 mph by the half mile mark, and would have to be running at 3000 revs to actually get off the ground. This meant that it was nearly as dangerous taking off with a maximum load, as it was flying to Berlin and back. And what we experienced, my friend and I, was a Lancaster flying directly over our heads at 3000 revs, having to lift a maximum load. You've probably never heard four Merlin engines running at their very best, but that's what we experienced; the ground vibrated and shook, and so did we. So you can understand why we never did that again, but it really was a once in a lifetime experience. I can't think of many other people who have had the same experience of lying under a Lancaster taking off at full capacity, flying straight over, only feet above you.

So, as I was saying, we never missed watching the Lancasters taking off, or very rarely. I remember that the most Lancasters which took off from the airfield in one night was forty one planes, mixed from both squadrons, whereas usually it would be an average of twenty five to thirty two. If they were going on a mission deep into Germany; Berlin, Nuremberg, Munich, Leipzig, they would have to get airborne and circle the airfield in a circuit. They would need to reach 10,000 ft before they could set course for Germany and would be going round and round, climbing steadily to reach the required height in their circuit, which could take up to twenty or thirty minutes. When the Lancasters took off from East Kirkby at 3000 - 4000 ft, you could also look across to RAF Coningsby, which was only five miles as the crow flies and see their Lancasters climbing to 1500 - 2000 ft. Then, 207 squadron from RAF Spilsby, which was another five miles away, could be seen climbing too, from 2000 - 3000 ft. You could also look towards RAF Woodhall, Scampton, Dunholme Lodge, Waddington, and see all their Lancasters on a clear night. In fact, if you looked towards any of the airfields on the Lincolnshire side of the Humber, you would see all their Lancasters becoming airborne. East Kirkby Squadrons would be flying in a circuit, Coningsby and Spilsby would be flying in another direction and so on and so on with each circuit in a different direction so they could all see one another, and you know I never saw one collision! If you looked directly up at East Kirkby airfield you would see all the Lancasters climbing higher and you would look into the distance and the sky would look absolutely full of Lancasters. I've heard it said like this before and it truly would have been. To give you an idea of what the scene would look like, on the road outside the airfield there would be families, friends, brothers, sisters, mothers and fathers and all the locals, sitting in chairs and leaning on fences, all gathered to watch this panorama of Lancasters. Then, all of a sudden, after all this noisy time of Lancasters climbing into the air, I might be talking to somebody, and they were just gone. Everything would just go quiet. Then we would begin to make our way back up the hill to Old Bolingbroke and I would be thinking to myself, "I wonder where they're all going tonight and how many of them will be coming back." That's how we used to think. As the planes returned to the airfield after their operations, the majority of the time they would wake you up. Obviously, they would return in the middle of the night so you would be asleep, but when they returned they were much lower and their engines had a totally different sound. You see, on their way up the engines were struggling and they were going with much higher revs, but on their way back in, all the bombs had been dropped and fuel used, so they were running on lower revs. It was more of a true noise of the Rolls Royce Merlin engines because they weren't labouring. Because of this, and how low down they were, we would only hear East Kirkby Squadrons landing and wouldn't be able to hear the Lancasters from surrounding airfields close by.

I would just like to say something on the personnel who worked there. When East Kirkby Airfield first opened there would have been at least 2,700 Airmen and WAAFs, aircrew and ground crew. The ground crew, as far as I'm concerned, were the salt of the Earth, because when we used to go and watch these Lancasters taking off, sometimes we would go down to the airfield and stand at the end of the runway, hoping that they would take off these particular nights. The only way that we knew for sure that they were going to do so, would be when we saw one of the crew buses coming onto the airfield and dropping seven men off at each aircraft, which would let us know that they would be starting very soon and there would be great activity on the airfield from the ground staff. We would also know because there would be a lorry with black and white checked walls, which would arrive at the end of the runway and a man would come to the lorry and give the green light for take-off. The airfield would suddenly become bustling with great activity and the Lancasters would begin to start their engines up; 57 squadron and 630 squadron. They would have 57 squadron on one side of the airfield and 630 squadron would be stationed on the other and when they began leaving the dispersal, coming out onto the perimeter track and taxiing up to the end of the runway ready to take off, everything would be very well planned. You would probably get anything between ten and fifteen Lancasters on the perimeter track from 57 squadron and the same number from 630 squadron. A Lancaster from 57 would get lined up at the end of the runway, the black and white caravan would give him the green light to go and the pilot would give the engines full revs and then let it go down the runway. Next, a 630 Lancaster would turn into the main runway and he would be given the green light for take-off and so on with a 57 Lancaster, then a 630 Lancaster, 57, and so on. They all used to do this, instead of letting one squadron go in full, then the next, in order to keep the engines cool. Then all the ground crew would begin to make their way to the billets and probably rest after the day's work of getting the Lancasters ready for operation from the early morning to late night. Some of them would come back again early next morning to see if the Lancaster that they looked after had come back again. There would be six to eight men per aircraft to keep it in flying condition and I always admired the ground crew and the WAAF drivers because they would work all the hours that were available to keep their planes in flying condition. Time didn't matter to them and they would work in all weathers; wind, snow and rain to service their planes. Even during the winter time, from January to March, with the wind coming in from the North East and with snow on the ground, they would work outside all the time.

They never took Lancasters inside the hangars unless it was major service work, it would always be done on the airfield in dispersal. During the winter months, they didn't have very good clothing; just wellington boots, white stockings and leather jerkins. They would be working all day and all night if need be. They would be putting bombs into the bomb bays, servicing the engines and filling the petrol tanks up with fuel as soon as they arrived home from a bombing raid, which could be anywhere from 2 o'clock until 5 o'clock in the morning. The ground crew used to think a lot of their aircraft and if one failed to return from a mission, they really would be upset over it because they wouldn't know whether it had been shot down or whether it was due to mechanical fault. In the winter months when they were doing their repair work, their fingers would be numb cold, from bicycling from billet to billet, shovelling snow from aircraft wings ready to go on their raids. The whole airfield would be a hive of activity, twenty four hours a day, day in and day out. All the airfield personnel were conscious of the many dangers the aircrew were facing. I know for a fact, that there was one particular airman, who was one of the seven man ground crew who looked after one of the Lancasters, that when all the Lancasters had taken off and gone to Germany, even if he was on his bicycle on his way back to his billet, he would always stop and go down on his knees to pray for the safe journey back to East Kirkby. Now, this would have taken a lot of doing in front of all of his mates, but that was the spirit in those days, it was very serious when it came to that, and I cannot speak highly enough of the aircrew who took part in Bomber Command. In my opinion, the aircrew were the cream of the country and the ground crew were the salt of the Earth.

I mentioned earlier about my brother, Chris, joining the ATC at Worksop and when we came back to Lincolnshire to Old Bolingbroke in 1942, Chris volunteered for aircrew at Worksop. He was accepted and began training to be a flight engineer, passing out in 1943. It took six to nine months training to qualify as a flight engineer, so he was flying by late 1943. Chris was placed on Halifax bombers, which were similar to Lancasters with four engines. He was crewed up from Topcliffe in Yorkshire and was trained specifically for Halifax bombers, because he, like all aircrew, didn't have a choice as to the aircraft they would be trained for and would be automatically assigned to their plane.

Chris would probably come home on leave an average of every six or seven weeks, whenever he could really. I would nearly always go and meet him as he came off the Lincolnshire bus and then walk him back again, just to get as much time with him as possible. After Chris had started his tour of operations, we noticed how he seemed to age overnight. He grew up and matured quickly, as did all the young men who fought during the war; they were bound to, with all the responsibility that they had and the experiences they faced during their service.

My brother was flying with Canadians and he started his tour of operations with 405 Squadron, then 419 Squadron in Middle Saint George and then to 433 Squadron at Skipton-on-Swale, North Yorkshire. We used to watch the Lancasters taking off from East Kirby from August 1943, which was the same date as the beginning of Chris' tour of operations. I was then at the age to understand the dangers which were involved, the dangers that my brother, Chris, was involved in. Whenever the Lancasters were leaving, I used to think, "I bet Chris is going tonight," and he nearly always was. So seeing them take off always used to make us think of Chris and the one night that we didn't think of him was the night that Chrissy went missing. He had been shot down over Nuremberg and if he had returned from that mission, he would have completed his tour of operations. On that night we lost ninety four Lancaster and Halifax Bombers.

Chris's Days in the RAF

Chris joins the RAF   Chris at home on leave at Old Bolingbroke

Chris in Yorkshire with his Halifax

Chapter Four

Losing Brother Chris

The night that we lost bother Chris, on the Nuremberg raid on the 31st March 1944, we lost ninety four aircraft; Lancaster and Halifax bombers. We heard on the seven o'clock news the next morning that Bomber Command had paid a visit to Nuremberg the night before, and that many of our bombers were missing. That raid was the heaviest loss that Bomber Command and families across the World endured on any night during the War. There were over five hundred airmen killed that night.

I shall never forget that, as I have already said, whenever the bombers were taking off from East Kirkby, we always used to think, "I bet Chrissie will be going tonight, from Skipton-on-Swale," but, for some reason or other, that night, when Chris went over Nuremburg, the family didn't think about him going and that was the night that we lost him. And the saddest part of it is that this raid was Chrissie's last mission before he completed his tour of operations.

I remember the lad who brought the telegram to us at our home in Old Bolingbroke. He was called Maurice Fenwick. We used to sit at the same desk at school and his mother owned the Post Office. Maurice brought the telegram on the 2nd April 1944, to let us know that Chris had failed to return from the previous night's operation. Our house was on the side of the road and I was playing in the middle of the road when Maurice rode up to me on his bicycle. We were on the slope of quite a steep hill, so he had to climb off his bicycle and push it up the last part of the hill to get to us. Maurice's first words to me were, "Are your mother and father in, Fred?" and I just said, "Yes, they are Maurice." I noticed that he had a buff coloured envelope in his hand and wondered what this telegram was, although I could almost guess. He didn't say another word to me and I watched him as he walked up the pathway to the house and knocked on the front door. My mother answered and she took the telegram upstairs to Father because he was in bed with the flu, under the Doctor's instructions. I was still standing across the road, just looking at the door. I watched as my father came down the stairs in his pyjamas and sat down in his chair by the coal fire and I could see that he was very upset and crying. I knew then that it was definitely something about Chris having failed to come back from a night operation and I just daren't go up into the house at the time. So I ran across a small field to the farm and I sat down on a tumbrel in the crew yard where the cattle were and I sat there for a really long time. I daren't go back because I knew what had happened. It was a quarter to six when the telegram came and I had been sitting in the crew yard, on this tumbrel, until gone nine o'clock at night, because I just didn't want to return home. Eventually, I came to the conclusion that I would have to go back because Mother and Father would be wondering where I was. That night is still as vivid to me today as it was back then.

Eventually, I did return home and I can say at this point that my father took a long while; many, many years, before he really got over it. I remember that at the time, I had to go to the post office every morning to see if there were any letters or telegrams about my brother, because Father couldn't wait until the post was delivered at ten o'clock in the morning. So I had to be at Mavis Enderby post office, which was a mile away, at half past seven in the morning to take the post to Father who was working in the field and then I would walk back to get to school. And I did that every morning for four months, for my father.

I remember that one particular morning, around four months after the telegram had been delivered by Maurice, a letter came from the Red Cross. It had been forwarded by the Ministry, but the Red Cross had received it because they were in parts of Europe doing the research for information for families of the bereaved and they got the news from German information. They had found the wreckage of my brother's Halifax and the five members of the crew who had lost their lives. There had been eight members of the crew that night and the three who had bailed out safely were:

Jack McClauchlan the Rear Gunner, Canadian.
Harry Cooper the Wireless Operator, Canadian.
Christian Nielsen the Pilot, Danish.

The five men who lost their lives were:

Awrey, the Navigator, Canadian.
Thompson, the Mid-Upper Gunner, Irish.
Milward, the Bomb Aimer, Canadian.
C. W. Panton, the Flight Engineer, English.
Rost, the second pilot in training, Canadian.

Rost had gone that night with an experienced crew before he started his tour of operations, which is what new pilots would do before they started their own tours, so they could see what it was like flying with a senior crew.

I used to stay with Father every morning until he had opened the letters and read the contents. So he read the names of the three survivors out to me and we really hoped that Chris would be one of them, but it wasn't meant to be. Then he read the names of the men who had lost their lives and the information that had been given to the Red Cross by German Information. After reading that letter I didn't have to go to the post office in the morning anymore. It was a very, very sad time, as you can imagine, but my family always thought that if anything happened to Chrissie, then Mother would never get over it. But it was just the opposite. Father took the news very, very badly, but Mother hardly showed any of her feelings. She covered them up for my father; she had to be strong for him and for her family.

Between where we used to go to school and where we lived was an avenue of big Elm trees, around twenty metres apart from each other. Before we received that letter, my brother Harold would say to me that if he could run to the next tree in so many strides, then Chrissie was still alive and, you know, he always managed to do it in the number of strides that he said he could. So we would think that Chris was still alive and that would make us feel a lot better. He did that so many times and he always did it in the number of strides that he challenged himself.

Christopher in training in Yorkshire

Topcliffe Airfield June, 1943
Left to right back row: Don Awrey, Navigator; Jack McLauchlan, Rear gunner;
Harry Cooper, Wireless operator/Air gunner; Leo Milward, Bomb aimer
Front row: Chris Panton, Flight engineer; Chris Nielsen, Pilot

Chapter 5

Keeping in Touch

Letter from Fred's Father:

> Old Bolingbroke Road
> Mavis Enderby
> 27. 3. 44.   Spilsby.
>
> Dear Son Chrissie.
>
> you will think I
> have been taking my time in writing
> but I have been ill (Had Bronchitis)
> & have been in bed. I am still under
> the Dr. although I am much better &
> still under improving. I am sorry to
> keep you waiting for a letter but I
> don't seem to have had the energy
> to write even. I thank you for your
> letter & I find the Newspaper cuttings
> very interesting indeed. Good luck to
> him. Berlin must have been a hot
> place on Sat night Was you there I
> wondered about you & all the boys
> when we heard & saw them going.
> By jove there was some went over
> here. We were pleased to get your
> letter I am enclosing the coupons in.

27.3.44
Dear Son Chrissie.

*You will think I have been taking my time in writing but I have been ill
(bronchitis) I have been in bed. I am still under the Dr. although I am much
better and still improving. I am sorry to keep you waiting for a letter but I
don't seem to have had the energy to write even. I thank you for your letter
and I find the newspaper cuttings very interesting indeed. Good luck to him.
Berlin must have been a hot place on Sat night, was you there? I wondered
about you and all the boys when we heard and saw them going. By jove
there was some went over here. We were pleased to get your letter, I am
enclosing the coupons in*

Unfortunately the last part of the letter has been lost over time and this is the
only half remaining. This is the very last letter that my Father sent to
Chrissie, which he did not receive. The letter was dated just five days before
my brother was lost in the Nuremberg raid. The letter was in Chrissie's
locker, awaiting his return from his last mission, which would have
completed his tour of operations. Along with my Father's last letter to him
was a letter of his commission, from his previous position of Sergeant to
Pilot Officer. He never received this title in writing before he lost his life
either.

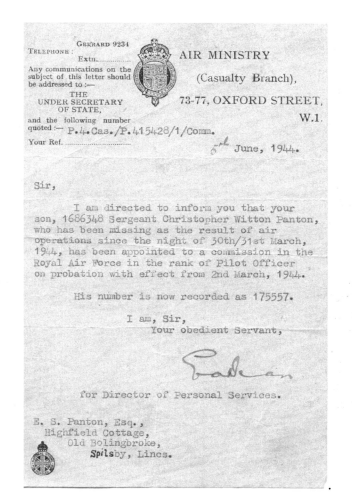

5th June 1944

Sir,

I am directed to inform you that your son, 1686348 Sergeant Christopher Whitton Panton, who has been missing as a result of air operations since the night of 30th/31st March, 1944, has been appointed to a commission in the Royal Air Force in the rank of Pilot Officer on probation with effect from 2nd March, 1944.

His number is now recorded as 175557.

I am sir,
Your obedient Servant.

BUCKINGHAM PALACE

The Queen and I offer you our heartfelt sympathy in your great sorrow.

We pray that your country's gratitude for a life so nobly given in its service may bring you some measure of consolation.

George R.I.

E. S. Panton, Esq.

Buckingham Palace.

The Queen and I offer you our heartfelt sympathy in your great sorrow.

We pray that your Country's gratitude for a life so nobly given in its service may bring you some measure of consolation.

George R.I

President :
HER MAJESTY THE QUEEN

Grand Prior :
H.R.H. THE DUKE OF GLOUCESTER, K.G.

WOUNDED, MISSING AND RELATIVES DEPARTMENT

Chairman : THE DOWAGER LADY AMPTHILL, C.I., G.B.E.

Telephone No.
SLOANE 9696

In replying please quote reference :
S/MFE/RAF/C.11900

**7 BELGRAVE SQUARE,
LONDON, S.W.1**

26th May, 1944.

Dear Mrs. Panton,

      We very much regret to have to tell you
that no information has come through attached to
the name of your son, Sergeant C.Panton, No.1686348,
although full enquiries are being made on your behalf.
We feel it is only right, however, that you should
be informed of the grievous report which has reached
us through the International Red Cross Committee
at Geneva, concerning the crew of which your son was
a member, for although the information which this
contains can but add most deeply to your already
great anxiety, we believe that you would not wish
it to be withheld.

      A telegram from the Organisation at Geneva
reports that according to the official German
authorities, five airmen lost their lives on the
31st March, 1944, but at the time when this report
came through their names had not then been ascertained
by the enemy. The further information was included
that Pilot Officer C. Nielsen, Warrant Officer First-
Class H.Cooper, and Warrant Officer Second-Class
J.G.McLaughlin were taken prisoner. We fear that
until further information is forthcoming, no official
action can be taken about the above five airmen
whose lives are stated to have been lost, one of whom
is your son, and these airmen must still remain

classified as "Missing".

                       P.T.O.

We realise what this report will mean to you, and we wish you to know that every effort is being made in order to clarify this distressing situation.

We are endeavouring to get into touch with the airmen taken prisoner, and should we eventually succeed in obtaining any helpful additional news from this source we shall of course communicate with you again. We are sure you will understand, however, that our enquiries to Prisoners of War are now very much delayed.

Please understand that whenever further information comes to light you will be notified immediately, and we ask you to accept meanwhile our sympathy in the great sorrow this letter must bring to you.

Yours sincerely,

Margaret Ampthill

Chairman.

Mr. A.S.Fanton,
Old Bolingbroke Road,
Mavis Enderby,
Spilsby.
Lincs.

WAR ORGANISATION
OF THE

BRITISH RED CROSS SOCIETY and ORDER OF ST. JOHN OF JERUSALEM

WOUNDED, MISSING AND RELATIVES DEPARTMENT

Dear Mrs. Panton,

We very much regret to have to tell you that no information has come through attached to the name of your son, Sergeant C. Panton, No. 1686348, although full enquiries are being made on your behalf. We feel it is only right, however, that you should be informed of the grievous report which has reached us through the International Red Cross Committee at Geneva, concerning the crew of which your son was a member, for although the information which this contains can but add most deeply to your already great anxiety, we believe you would not wish it to be withheld.

A telegram from the Organisation at Geneva reports that according to the official German authorities, five airmen lost their lives on the 31st March 1944, but at the time when this report came through their names had not been ascertained by the enemy. The further information was included the Pilot Officer C. Nielsen, Warrant Officer First-Class H. Cooper, and warrant Officer Second-Class J. G. McClauchlan were taken prisoner. We fear that until further information is forthcoming, no official action can be taken about the above five airmen whose lives are stated to have been lost, one of whom is your son, and these airmen must still remain classified as "Missing".

We realise what this report will mean to you, and we wish you to know that every effort is being made in order to clarify this distressing situation.

We are endeavouring to get into touch with the airmen taken prisoner, and should we eventually succeed in obtaining any helpful additional news from this source we shall of course communicate with you again. We are sure you will understand, however, that our enquiries to Prisoners of War are now very much delayed.

Please understand that whenever further information comes to light you will be notified immediately, and we ask you to accept meanwhile our sympathy in the great sorrow this letter must bring to you.

Yours sincerely,

ADVICE TO THE RELATIVE
OF A MAN WHO IS MISSING

In view of the official notification that your relative is missing, you will naturally wish to hear what is being done to trace him.

The Service Departments make every endeavour to discover the fate of missing men, and draw upon all likely sources of information about them.

A man who is missing after an engagement may possibly be a prisoner of war. Continuous efforts are made to speed up the machinery whereby the names and camp addresses of prisoners of war can reach this country. The official means is by lists of names prepared by the enemy Government. These lists take some time to compile, especially if there is a long journey from the place of capture to a prisoners of war camp. Consequently "capture cards" filled in by the prisoners themselves soon after capture and sent home to their relatives are often the first news received in this country that a man is a prisoner of war. That is why you are asked in the accompanying letter to forward at once any card or letter you may receive, if it is the first news you have had.

Even if no news is received that a missing man is a prisoner of war, endeavours to trace him do not cease. Enquiries are pursued not only among those who were serving with him, but also through diplomatic channels and the International Red Cross Committee at Geneva.

The moment reliable news is obtained from any of these sources it is sent to the Service Department concerned. They will pass the news on to you at once, if they are satisfied that it is reliable. It would be cruel to raise false hopes, such as may well be raised if you listen to one other possible channel of news, namely, the enemy's broadcasts. These are listened to by official listeners, working continuously night and day. The few names of prisoners given by enemy announcers are carefully checked. They are often misleading, and this is not surprising, for the object of the inclusion of prisoners' names in these broadcasts is not to help the relatives of prisoners, but to induce British listeners to hear some tale which otherwise they could not be made to hear. The only advantage of listening to these broadcasts is an advantage to the enemy.

The official listeners can never miss any name included in an enemy broadcast. They pass every name on to the Service Department concerned. There every name is checked, and in every case where a name can be verified, the news is sent direct to the relatives.

There is, therefore, a complete official service designed to secure for you and to tell you all discoverable news about your relative. This official service is also a very human service, which well understands the anxiety of relatives and will spare no effort to relieve it.

7-43 (20352) 57995/M4040 10,000 3/44 K.H.K. Gp. 8/8

Advice to the relative of a man who is missing

In view of the official notification that your relative is missing, you will naturally wish to hear what is being done to trace him.

The service departments make every endeavour to discover the fate of missing men, and draw upon all likely sources of information about them.

A man who is missing after an engagement may possibly be a prisoner of war. Continuous efforts are made to speed up the machinery whereby the names and camp addresses of prisoners of war can reach this Country. The official means is by lists of names prepared the enemy Government. These lists take some time to compile, especially if there is a long journey from the place of capture to a prisoner of war camp. Consequently "capture cards" filled in by the prisoners themselves soon after capture and sent home to their relatives are often the first news received in this Country that a man is a prisoner of war. That is why you are asked in the accompanying letter to forward at once any card of letter you may receive, if it is the first news you have had.

Even if no news is received that a missing man is a prisoner of war, endeavours to trace him do not cease. Enquiries are pursued not only among those who were serving with him, but also through diplomatic channels and the International Red Cross Committee at Geneva.

The moment reliable news is obtained from any of these sources it is sent to the Service Department concerned. They will pass the news on to you at once, if they are satisfied that it is reliable. It would be cruel to raise false hopes, such as may well be raised if you listen to one other possible channel of news, namely, the enemy's broadcasts. These are listened to by official listeners, working continuously night and day. The few names of prisoners given by enemy announcers are carefully checked. They are often misleading, and this is not surprising, for the object of the inclusion of prisoner' names in the broadcasts is not to help the relatives of prisoners, but to induce British listeners to hear some tale which otherwise they could not be made to hear. The only advantage of listening to these broadcasts is an advantage of the enemy.

The official listeners can never miss any name included in an enemy broadcast. They pass every name on to the Service Department concerned. There every name is checked, and in every case where a name can be verified, the news is sent direct to the relatives.

There is, therefore, a complete official service designed to secure for you and to tell you all discoverable news about your relative. This official service is also a very human service, which well understands the anxiety of relatives and will spare no effort to relieve it.

SUPREME HEADQUARTERS
ALLIED EXPEDITIONARY FORCE

Soldiers, Sailors and Airmen of the Allied Expeditionary Force!

You are about to embark upon the Great Crusade, toward which we have striven these many months. The eyes of the world are upon you. The hopes and prayers of liberty-loving people everywhere march with you. In company with our brave Allies and brothers-in-arms on other Fronts, you will bring about the destruction of the German war machine, the elimination of Nazi tyranny over the oppressed peoples of Europe, and security for ourselves in a free world.

Your task will not be an easy one. Your enemy is well trained, well equipped and battle-hardened. He will fight savagely.

But this is the year 1944! Much has happened since the Nazi triumphs of 1940-41. The United Nations have inflicted upon the Germans great defeats, in open battle, man-to-man. Our air offensive has seriously reduced their strength in the air and their capacity to wage war on the ground. Our Home Fronts have given us an overwhelming superiority in weapons and munitions of war, and placed at our disposal great reserves of trained fighting men. The tide has turned! The free men of the world are marching together to Victory!

I have full confidence in your courage, devotion to duty and skill in battle. We will accept nothing less than full Victory!

Good Luck! And let us all beseech the blessing of Almighty God upon this great and noble undertaking.

Dwight D. Eisenhower

Supreme Headquarters Allied Expeditionary Force

Soldiers, Sailors and Airmen of the Allied Expeditionary Force!

You are about to embark upon the Great Crusade, toward which we have striven these many months. The eyes of the world are upon you. The hopes and prayers of liberty-loving people everywhere march with you. In company with our brave Allies and brothers-in-arms on other fronts, you will bring about the destruction of the German war machine, the elimination of Nazi tyranny over the oppressed peoples of Europe, and security for ourselves in a free world.

Your task will not be an easy one. Your enemy is well trained, well equipped and battle-hardened. He will fight savagely.

But this is the year 1944! Much has happened since the Nazi triumphs of 1940-41. The United Nations have inflicted upon the Germans great defeats, in open battle, man-to-man. Our air offensive has seriously reduced their strength in the air and their capacity to wage war on the ground. Our Home Fronts have given us an overwhelming superiority in weapons and munitions of war, and placed at our disposal great reserves of trained fighting men. The tide has turned! The free men of the world are marching together to Victory!

I have full confidence in your courage, devotion to duty and skill in battle. We will accept nothing less than full Victory!

Good luck! And let us all beseech the blessing of Almighty God upon his great and noble undertaking.

Dwight Eisenhower

Letters from Chris:

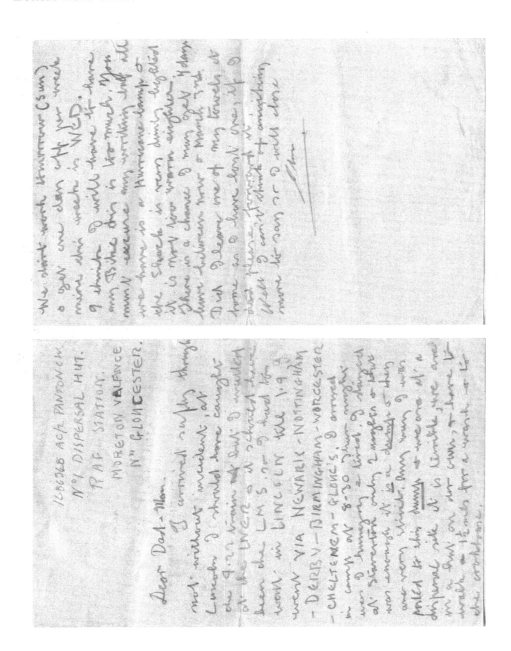

Dear Dad and Mam,

I arrived safely though not without incident, at Lincoln I should have caught the 9.22 train but I waited at the LNER and it should have been the LMS. So I had to wait in LINCOLN till 1.9 I went VIA NEWARK-NOTTINGHAM-DERBY-BIRMINGHAM-WORCESTER-CHELTENHAM-GLOUC's. I arrived in camp at 8.30 that night. [I was] hungry and tired. I stayed at Staverton only 2 nights and that was enough it is a dump and they are very strict. Anyway I was posted to this dump and we are at a dispersal site. It is terrible, we are in a hut on our own, I have to walk 1 ½ miles for a wash and to the {.........?} We start work tomorrow (Sun) and get one day off per week. Mine this week is WED.

I think I will have to have my bike, this is too much. You must excuse my writing but all we have is a Hurricane lamp and the spark is very dimly lighted. It is not too warm either. There is a chance I may get 7 days leave between now and March 3rd. Did I leave one of my towels at home as I have lost one, if I did please forward it.

Well I can't think of anything more to say so I will close

Chris.

1680348 A/c2 PANTON.
Hut B4.

A squadron 2 wing
R.A.F. Locking
Weston-s-Mare.
Somerset.

Dear Mam & Dad,

Just a line to let
you know I am keeping well as I
hope this finds you, how are Fred &
Harold I bet they are mischevous. Is
dad catching many rabbits, tell him to
leave me some for me to shoot when
I get home, it won't be long now
you know. I am getting on pretty well
with my course finish working on
Pegasus & Hercules on Thursday & then
start on Kestrel & Merlin. In line
Engines. Yor as you can see I am
getting rather Technically Minded.

I have took all the Engines down I have been on so far + off course assembled them. I believe I could strip + assemble a motor-car engine 10 H.P. when I can + a Hercules 1000 H.P. I have passed quite a few stages so far, Mainly, Basic, Preliminary Engine Magneto's, Carburretters, Air cooled Engines + am now going onto Liquid Cooled Engines, I have to do after Liquid Cooled Eng's, Components, Installation + Aerodrome Procedure. So you can see I have completed at least half of my course. Will you please send me that book, The Morse Code as I do wireless in my spare time, I also go to Maths Classes. I am enjoying myself immensely on this camp. Of course it has its snags, for instance

Guard Duties, I am on, today (Saturday) it won't be too bad though as I am on the Patrol. I had an Electric shock when we were on Magneto's having a dose of 14,000 volts go through me my arms still ache,(a month after). I'm not so keen on them now I might tell you I can't explain the feeling but it is as if you were suddenly lifted up + dropped again.(an experience I won't forget). 168 entrees (my entree) had 48 hr leave last Weekend I didn't take mine instead I had it put on my 7 days which I get in January. We had a few bombs at Weston the other night. What do you think to the news from Egypt. Please remember the Morse Code, Book. Your Son
Chris.

1686348 A/C 2 PANTON.
Hut B4
A Squadron 2 wing
R.A.F. Locking
Weston-S-Mare
Somerset

Dear Mam & Dad,

Just a line to let you know I am keeping well as I hope this finds you, how are Fred & Harold, I bet they are mischievous. Is Dad catching many rabbits, tell him to leave me some for me to shoot when I get home, it won't be long now you know. I am getting on pretty well with my course finish working on Pegasus & Hercules on Thursday & then start on Kestrel & Merlin. In line Engines. Yes as you can see I am getting rather technically minded. I have [taken] the engines down I have been on so far & off course assembled them. I believe I could strip & assemble a motor-car engine 10 HP when I can a Hercules 1000HP.I have passed quite a few stages so for, mainly, basic, preliminary engine magnetoes, carburettors, air-cooled engines & am now going onto liquid-cooled engines, I have to do after liquid-cooled engine's, components, installation & aerodrome procedure. So you can see I have completed at least half of my course. Will you please send me that book, The Morse Code as I do wireless in my spare time, I also go to maths classes. I am enjoying myself immensely on this camp. Of course it has its stages, for instance guard duties, I am on today (Saturday) it won't be too bad though as I am on the patrol. I had an electric shock when we were on magnetoes having a dose of 14,000 volts go through me. My arms still ache, (a month after). I'm not so keen on them now I might tell you I can't explain the feeling but it is as if you were suddenly lifted up and dropped again (an experience I won't forget). 168 entrée (my entrée) had 48 hours leave last weekend I didn't take mine instead I had it put on my 7 days which I get in January. We had a few bombs at Weston the other night. What do you think to the news from Egypt. Please remember the Morse Code book.

Your Son

Chris.

Dear Folks,
I thought you might like to know I have moved a little nearer as you will no doubt admit. I have been here since Monday and am enjoying things tremendously. We are free to walk around the town but [there] is a 2 mile limit. I will see if I can't get home sometime, although the odds are against it, we are here only for 5 weeks doing 8 weeks training in that time, so you can imagine we have to work, but we don't mind that as it is interesting. The reason I did not write as soon as I came was because I had and still have not any money to pay the postage, I had to borrow this. Will you please look in the pockets of my clothes and see if I have left a £1 note in them as I appear to have lost one. I presume my clothes arrived, if so if the £1 is in them please send it along with my mouth-organ to the above address as soon as possible, as I am on the rocks till next pay day and I don't know when that will be. I am billeted in the Windsor hotel along the sea front road. I have a bedroom of my own in which is a wash basin, hot and cold water and an electric light, so you will agree I am lucky. Please don't be long writing back as it is an unenviable position to see other chaps receiving mail and me not. Our work here is square-bashing, musketry, grenade-throwing and all such duties. Our real training does not come in till we get posted again. Tomorrow (Saturday) is rather a new experience for me; inoculation & vaccination, something to look forward to. Have had two more medicals since I came and a dental in which I was again pronounced fit and well. I don't think there is anything more so I will close, remember to answer quickly and get the address correctly, this is important.

Your son Chris

Send Evelyn's address please.

1686348 SGT. PANTON.

29/2/44

SGT'S MESS R.A.F.

SKIPTON - ON - SWALE

YORKS.

Dear Mam & Dad,

Having a little line to spare I decided it was about time I wrote to you very sorry I have been so long in writing.

Are you all keeping well. I hope so. Myself I have not been too well lately having a sore throat, (swollen tonsils I believe) & having a patch of impetigo on my left knee. But right now I feel much better.

I was very pleased to hear my snares caught 2 more rabbits & hope you will have good catches there last weeks this season. We have had a fairly heavy fall of snow up here recently but now again it is almost gone.

49

Today I spent three hrs flying at
24000 ft with the temperature 45°C below
Zero, it was really cold. It was the
first time I have been so high in
daylight: everything looked so small, the
river Thames appeared the size of a line
on the palm of your hand. You will no
doubt be interested to hear I have now
over 350 flying hrs to my credit
& I have the highest number of
ops in my section to my credit. I have
now only nine more to do having finished
me 22nd when we went to SCHWEINFURT.
I have also been to Berlin & Leipzig
since I came off leave (Leipzig was deadly).
I'll have a number of stories to tell
you when I come on leave again &
also something to show you.

I have heard my crown is through but I have not heard officially yet. My Commission papers were put in a fortnight ago but I am very doubtful as to whether I will get it.

Incidentally I will be home on leave the sixth of March (6 weeks time) reason unknown period. I hope Evelyn will be able to get...

What do you think to the Habby III. Don't you think its a very nice sleek looking aircraft. Well I'm afraid I must close the time is 7.10 (just to let you know the watch is still going strong. Until next Tuesday I wish you the best of luck & health.

From Chris

29/2/44

Dear Mam & Dad,

Having a little time to spare I decided it was about time I wrote to you. Very sorry I have been so long in writing.

Are you all keeping well, I hope so. Myself, I have not been too well lately having a sore throat, (swollen tonsils I believe & having a patch of impetigo on my left….? But right now I feel much better.

I was very pleased to hear my snares caught 2 more rabbits and hope you will have good catches these last weeks this season. We have had a fairly heavy fall of snow up here recently but now again it is almost gone.

Today I spent three hours flying at 24,000 ft with the temperature 45 ℃ below zero, it was really cold. It was the first time I have been so high in daylight, everything looked so small, the river Humber appeared the size of a line in the palm of your hand. You will no doubt be interested to hear I have now over 350 flying hrs to my credit & I have the highest number of ups in my section to my credit. I have now only nine more to do having finished the 22ⁿᵈ when we went to SCHWEINFURT. I have been to Berlin & Leipzig since I came off leave (Leipzig was deadly).

I'll have a number of stories to tell you when I get leave again & also something to show you. I have heard my crown is through but I have not heard officially yet. My commission papers were put in a fortnight ago but I am very doubtful as to whether I will get it.

Incidentally I will be home on leave the sixth of March (a week's time) ……? …….? Period. I hope Evelyn will be able to get.

What do you think to the Hally 3 (Halifax version 3) Don't you think it's a very nice sleek looking aircraft.

Well I'm afraid I must close the time is 7.10 just to let you know the watch is still going strong. Until next Tuesday I wish you the best of good health.

From Chris

23 - 5 - 44.

Dear Lynn,

It was quite a pleasant surprise to find a letter awaiting me when I docked though the mail pile today. It was quite a good letter so now write. The now all Sunkers will be off Great Camera St. I hope so. Sorry you have so much work to do. My Pilot Officer has gotten his Commission he is now a P O (Pilot Officer). I hope mind he came through before long. I have only been...

...2 that time I am but on leave + now hope I don't only 5 more to do. I am sending a Photograph of over but now. I arnest Millward here for short. He is only a short goes around S ft 5 inches tall. Will you tell Mum + Dad have it when you have finished so I want to keep that photo. So I write this letter the time are just taking if you will write mail. I am not in it as I am having the day off.

You I am interested in knowing if you have got me to spare. I'm afraid you can't think of anything more to say so I will close.

From Eric XXXX,

I thank you for thinking of sending me a parcel. It will be lovely forward to it.

P.S. Sorry to hear Dad is ill.

1686348 SGT Panton
Sgt's Mess RAF
SKIPTON-ON-SWALE
YORKS

23-3-44

Dear Gwen,

It was quite a pleasant surprise to find a letter awaiting me when I looked through the mail pile today. It was quite a good letter you wrote. Are you all keeping well at Queen St (?) I hope so.

Sorry you have so much work to do. My pilot Chris Nielsen has gotten his commission, he is now a P O (Pilot Officer). I hope mine to come through before long. I have only been on 2 operations since I was last on leave and now hope I have only 5 more to do. I am enclosing a photograph of our bomb-aimer Leonard Millward, Leo for short. He is only 5 ft 5 inches tall. Will you let Mum and Dad have it when you have finished as I want to keep that photo. As I write this letter the Lancs are just taking off for another raid. I am not in it as I am having the day off.

Yes I am interested in books if you have got one to spare. I'm afraid I can't think of anything more to say so I will close.

From Chris XXXXXXXXX

Thank you for thinking of sending me a parcel. I shall be looking forward to it.
P.S sorry to hear that Dad is ill.

This is the very last letter that Chris ever sent. It is particularly special to my family because in all of his other letters he would never close with any kisses, it wasn't his way. But in his last letter he put ten kisses; one for each of his brothers and sisters, Father and Mother. We all feel that he must have known that he wasn't going to make it; my sister told me that during his last visit on leave he really wasn't himself; he was very subdued and quiet with nothing to say, really, very unlike his usual character.

These are just a few of the letters that we received from Chris during the years that he was away in the Air Force. They only give a small idea of what life was like for them in service. You see Chris would hardly say anything about his missions or his experiences to us. He would only tell Dad a few things, which he selectively picked to tell him, when he came on leave; they would sit together in the sitting room, in front of the fire talking, whilst the rest of the family were upstairs in bed. My father was always keen to know what Chris was busy doing, he was very proud, and very worried about him, which you can imagine is normal for a Father.

The following letter is one sent by one of Chrissie's surviving crew members and best friends, the Rear-Gunner Jack McClauchlan, to my mother, after he had been released from the German Prisoner of War camp.

F/o McLACHLAN J.F.
J.86145 - E.P.O.W. - R.C.A.F.
3 P.R.C.
Bournemouth
Hants
28.5.45

My Dear Mrs Paton.

I hope you don't mind my writing this letter, but we were two of Chris's best friends. I had to write. You will probably remember me, as I was the Rear Gunner in Chris's crew.

You will probably want to know what happened to us on that fateful night of March 30th. We were about to run up on the target + all of a sudden a flame swept past my rear turret. Chris reported to the Skipper (Stewart Smith)

Engine on fire, Skipper. The Pilot tried unsuccessfully to extinguish the flames but to no avail. The Pilot then went in an uncontrollable dive which Nielson tried to remedy. He then told the crew to abandon aircraft fast. I did not waste any time, but I quickly jumped the hatch. No doubt you have heard who the survivors are. I just know they are:
P/o Nielson C. Pilot
P/o Cooper H. Wireless Op.
+ myself.

Chris Nielson + Harry Cooper were thrown through the side of the aircraft when it exploded at about 8,000 FOB. It was a terrible shock. They owe their lives I believe to the North as he must have helped them

What I cannot understand is
if the Lord helped Chris & they. Why didn't
to get killed & let your Chris escape
unwounded. If anyone had a right to live
it was their pardon. Chrissy would I have
laid my life down for Chris. He was the
truest friend I have ever had. I believe Chris
was the truest friend & had a boy I called
Benhurst nr WURNBURG we were not allowed
to talk the funeral & & spoke my heart.

At the time I went missing
no doubt Chris told you, I want him a found
not. So I have enclosed a postal order for
the sum.

Chris was always talking about
you his mother, sisters & two brothers

who was I shot was him when he was
on leave. He certainly did love you Mrs.
Carter and I would be proud of him.

He gave his life to protect people
who murdered. Your Chris more than has
like murdered. Save Chris the kind of a boy I wish
our vicar. He was the kid of a boy I wish
I could have been. Chris was my Pal!

I will finish off now. It was a
pleasure to know her a gallant, brave
chap as Chris. If I can ever do anything
for you I will help to his finish.

I remain,
Yours faithfully
Jack

P/O McClauchlan J.G.
J 86145 – X-P.O.W. – R.C.A.F.
3 P.R.C.
Bournemouth
Harts
28-5-45

My Dear Mrs Panton

    I hope you don't mind me writing Mrs Panton but as I was one of Chris's best friends I had to. You will probably remember me, as I was the Rear Gunner in Chris's crew.

    You will probably want to know what happened to us on that fateful night of March 30th. We were about to run up on the target and all of a sudden a flame swept past my rear turret. Chris reported to the Skipper, "Starboard Inner Engine on fire, Skipper". The pilot tried unsuccessfully to extinguish the flames but of no avail. The Plane then went in an uncontrollable dive in which Neilson could do nothing. He then told the crew to "Abandon Aircraft fast". I did not waste any time, but I went through the turret. No doubt you have heard who the survivors are, if not here they are.

P/O Nielsen C. – Pilot, P/O Cooper H. – Wireless Op, and myself.

    Chris Nielsen and Harry Cooper were blown through the side of the aircraft when it exploded at about 15,000 ft or so. It was a fluke; they owe their lives I believe to the Lord as he must have helped them.

    What I cannot understand is if the Lord helped Chris and Harry, why didn't I get killed and let Chris escape unscathed. If anyone had a right to live it was Chris Panton! Gladly I would have laid my life down for Chris. He was the truest friend I have ever had. I believe Chris will be buried around a town called Bamburgh near NURNBURG. We were not allowed to tend the funeral and it broke my heart.

    At the time I went missing, no doubt Chris told you, I owed him a pound note. So I have enclosed a postal order for the sum.

    Chris was always talking about his Mother and his wee brothers who used to shoot with him when he was on leave. He certainly did love you Mrs. Panton and I would be proud of him.

    He gave his life to protect people like ourselves. I owe Chris more than I can ever repay. He was the kind of a boy I wish I could have been. Chris was my Pal! I will finish off now. It was a pleasure to know such a gallant, brave chap as Chris. If I can ever do anything for you I will only be too pleased.

I remain
    Yours faithfully
       Jack

Chapter Six

Earwigs in Undergarments

Before going any further I would just like to tell you something of my elder sister, Evelyn, who I haven't mentioned before. Evelyn was in the Air Force. She volunteered in early 1941 to be in the WAAFs and after going through her course and drill, she was posted to a Spitfire Squadron in North Weald, near London, which I gather she liked very much. She has told me several times of her experiences at North Weald and she remarked one day that she remembered very well when the American Eagle Squadron came to North Weald. The Eagle squadron were classed as the elite and she would tell me what a nice bunch of pilots they were, as she got to know them. I think that Evelyn was involved in the Officers' Mess and she knew most of the pilots. She was telling me that when this Eagle Squadron first came, they didn't all have their proper uniforms, so they required some of the WAAFs to sew their brevvies on their tunics. Evelyn nearly always knew when a pilot had gone missing because there would be an empty table, which of course would be very sad. But she told me that in this Eagle Squadron, every single one of those men was eventually killed while they were flying. A Spitfire Squadron had twelve men and every one of those twelve planes was lost. But Evelyn enjoyed her years in the WAAFs, from 1941- 1946, until she was demobbed. She was a corporal and she could have stayed longer, but she declined because she was going to get married.

I want to tell you how she met her future husband. It was while we were living on the Osberton Estate, which, of course, I have mentioned several times before, and in the latter end of 1941, a searchlight arrived with a party of soldiers. It was half a mile from where we lived at Rayton Angles and I remember quite well when they came. There were about twenty soldiers, working the searchlight with some as cooks or mechanics. They used one of the brick buildings on a nearby farm for the cookhouse. This happened to be a dairy farm, run by a Mr Twidale, who was a tenant on the Osberton Estate. I was, of course, very interested in this searchlight that was going to be near us. I remember that I went down one night, around 5 o'clock when all the soldiers were there and the cook was just brewing them all a cup of tea in this big urn. While I was there, watching them all, the cook asked me if I would like a cup of tea and I said that I would and I am sure, even to this day, that that was one of the best cups of tea I have ever had in my life! So I often went down at their meal times to have a cup of tea and I could never work out why the soldiers of the army could make the best cups of tea you could have, because they really could.

As I mentioned before, we only lived sixteen miles from Sheffield, across country, in a keeper's cottage, which was surrounded by tall fir trees. Whenever they came to bomb Sheffield at night, my father would go outside and stand leaning on the fence at the side of the fir wood, where there was a gap in the hedge, looking towards Sheffield. There were many searchlights, which would be switched on, trying to find German aircraft. One particular night, when my father went out, our searchlight wasn't switched on yet, but as he watched, when it came on it was directly on a German aircraft. Of course, my father saw it and this German plane, having been spotted in the light, released its bombs immediately, before it got to Sheffield. The type of bombs that were dropped were called whistling bombs, because of the whistling noise that they made as they fell through the sky. And I can tell you that when you heard one of those bombs on its way down, whistling, it seemed to fall forever before it exploded through a building. It was terrifying hearing them, knowing they were so close, but not knowing where they would land. Father came running into the house on hearing these dropping bombs, with his head down. He opened the door and shouted up to us boys and girls, "Quick, get under the table or in the cupboard under the stairs; he's seen me!" The bombs, hitting the ground were only two fields away from where we lived. Father had said this German airplane had seen him, but of course it hadn't; it was pitch dark and he was inside this wood of tall fir trees! The person who was on duty on the light we called 'our searchlight', was going to be Evelyn's future husband. His name was Bill Pooley and he lived in London. How he came to meet my sister was, she came on leave, from North Wields and she had to walk from Worksop to Rayton Angles, which was about two miles. Of course, she would have to walk past this search battery to get back to the house and it was where one of the soldiers, Bill Pooley, saw her coming home on leave and that's where they met. After the war, when they were both demobbed they went to live in London. Bill joined the London police force until he retired and they had one boy and one girl together.

Now, I have another story of my sister Evelyn about her time in the services, but my good wife tells this story much better than I do because she had the first hand relay of this particular story, so I shall let her proceed.

"I have an amusing incident of Fred's sister, Evelyn, while she was in the WAAFs. She told me this story during a holiday I took with her around 1980, many years after the war. She was, as you know, stationed at North Wields and the WAAFs were all issued with government clothing, right down to their undergarments and they would store all their belongings in the lockers by the beds; that was the only place for them you see. Now, this particular Sunday morning, she was on RAF Church parade and Evelyn sat right at the front of the church, after they'd all marched in. They were, as I recall, at the Station Church and they were all expected to go to Sunday service, but they would usually try and find ways of getting out of it, if they could! So there she was, at the front of the congregation, when she started feeling nips and itches and this got progressively worse. She was wriggling and fidgeting, which of course was not allowed, in full view of her Commanding Officers. She tried to keep still, but it was so uncomfortable whilst she sat there in the service, that it was impossible for her to really sit still, as she was expected to. She just did not know what to do with herself! Eventually it became too uncomfortable for her and she had no alternative but to walk out of the service, even though she knew she would be reprimanded for doing such a thing.

So she had to stand in front of the Officer who wanted to know what the commotion was all about. Much to her horror she had to tell him everything; which ended up being earwigs in her knickers! Luckily, he saw the funny side of it and so she was not reprimanded. What had happened was these earwigs had been able to find a way into her locker and nestled into her knickers, and oh! If you had seen them! They were real knickers! You see, these were the government issued particulars, and they were huge, itchy things. They were so uncomfortable, even without the earwigs, that she used to hate wearing them. Since this incident they always undertook very thorough inspections to make sure there were no more repeat occasions! It was always a joke at the station after that and she was known as "Pants Panton", much to her disgust! If you could have heard her telling the story with such vigour, she had me in stitches!"

Evelyn in the RAF

Evelyn and friend

Chapter Seven

Run, Rabbit Run!

So now, it's 1944 and I'm thirteen years of age. My Father had trained me well on how to set rabbit snares and how to become a game keeper, so on Saturdays and holidays, I'd go keepering and snaring with him. During the wartime, my Father used to catch foxes and badgers, because during the wintertime, between December and March, you couldn't set traps because all the frost and snow on the ground would mean you wouldn't catch any rabbits. So what would happen is, you would be able to catch foxes or badgers instead, and a fox skin would be worth one pound and ten shillings, or you could catch a badger whose skin would be worth three pounds. This meant you would only need to catch one badger or fox through each winter week to keep a living, because catching a badger was the equivalent to one week's wage. By now, I would like to say that I was becoming more and more interested in the type of work that Father was doing. Anyway, my father was still working on the farm, gamekeeping and catching rabbits, as he always had done, when towards the latter end of 1944, November or December, he asked me what I was thinking of doing once I had left school. I said, "I want to work for myself and go into poultry farming. I want to be my own boss. That's what I really want to do." So he said, "Okay, if that's what you *really* want, I must start looking for a free house," which would mean moving house again, as we were at present living in a tied cottage, working on this farm. You see, a free house meant that you could live there and come and go as you like, you had no ties to the property. Eventually we found one at a place called Partney Watermill, so we moved back to Partney again in April 1945. Now, when we moved here I still had another three months to complete at school before I could leave, but I said to my father that I didn't think it was necessary to start another school again for only three months. So I actually finished school at thirteen years and three quarters, but of course, nothing was said of it in those days. Because I wanted to leave school and start my own business, which my father seemed to agree was a good idea, I left school and we did a full time job of rabbit catching together for farmers all around the district, and we were doing this from 1945 until 1949. We had a very large area of land to catch rabbits on, from Hareby, South Ormsby, Scrivelsby, West Keal and Grebby, near

Spilsby; all the small estates in the large surrounding area in Lincolnshire. After we were established in 1946, we engaged another lad to work with me by the name Jeff Lowie. Jeff was very interested in catching rabbits and proved to be a very good, hardworking lad and we all got on very well together and became good friends. And we still are to this day! I was running 220 snares which I used to set and move every two days, while my father would run rabbit traps. My younger brother, Harold, had also left school, so now he came to help with the rabbit catching and, of course, in those days there were lots of rabbits everywhere. They were in high demand because of the food shortages and meat rationing from the War. So Jeff Lowie used to carry the snares, while I would set them on the rabbit runs.

Now, setting snares is a very skilled job; you have to know just where to set the rabbit snare on the beat, which is the place where the rabbits would put their front feet or back feet. Once we had set all the snares, they would probably reach a mile and a half from the first snare to the last. It's the same process with setting a rabbit trap, knowing just where to put the trap in the hole of the burrow. You would glance at the hole before you set the trap and make sure that it looked the same again after you had moved the soil to set the trap. So there were four of us rabbit catching, and from September 1948 to the following March of 1949, which was known as rabbit season, (which is after the breeding season) we would catch rabbits until it was breeding season again. There were a lot of rabbits this particular year, in fact, as I recall, we were over-run with them. So we, my father and I, made our minds up that we would go all out and catch as many rabbits as humanly possible. Now I used to run a gross and a half of snares, which was two hundred and twenty snares, and my father and brother used to run one hundred and eighty traps. I would be able to average fifty couple rabbits every morning and my father could also average fifty couple in his traps. So we averaged one hundred couple of rabbits every morning during this rabbiting season. How we did it was; I moved my snares to a different ground every two days and Father also moved his traps onto another patch every two days. This meant very hard work, setting your traps and redoing them this often, but we did it to make sure we averaged those one hundred couple of rabbits every morning.

Whilst living at Partney, the local lads decided that we would like to start a football team, which everybody seemed to think was a good idea. So a gentleman of the name Mr Kime, who had been in the Navy during the

Second World War, had decided to put the team together. He went round all the lads in the village who he wanted to see in this team and I was one of the lads who was asked to play. After getting together, playing, and observing how everybody fitted together, we then had a team of lads, players in all the positions. I was put as centre forward and we joined the Skegness intermediate league. I played for three years while we were living at Partney Watermill and we all got on very well together and we won the league and the league cup for two years running. So I enjoyed my footballing days very much. You know, I don't think we realised how fit we were when we were young, you realise that when you get older; A lad called Tommy Hancock and myself, one time I recall, played three matches in one day! We played Wainfleet Town in the morning, Spilsby Town in the afternoon, and Nottingham Forest colts team at night; and we played full time at each match! I still have my football boots and shin guards that I wore in those days.

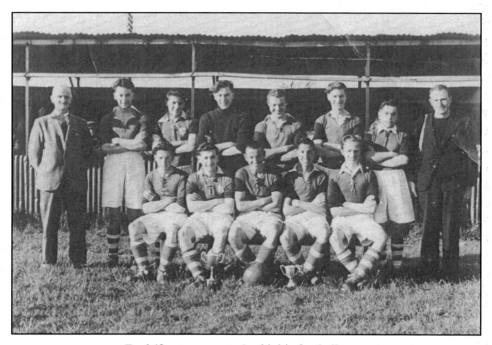

Fred (front row centre) with his football team

The Halifax Chris flew in ('N' Nielsen's Nuthouse)

Christian Nielsen (Pilot)

Chapter Eight

Nielsen's Respects

The truth about Chris

I would just like to point out here that when we moved to Partney in 1945, the war had not yet ended. The date it did end was May 8th 1945. Just going back to the War again, I remember that my brother's pilot came to see my father and mother and I remember this very well because we were digging the garden for the gentleman who used to buy all of our rabbits, a Mr Corney (Cornelius) Goodwin. We were in this big garden, Father and I and I just happened to stop and look round down the garden path and I said to my father, "There's an airman coming towards us," and then I looked again and I said, "He's a pilot," which I knew because he had his full set of World War Two wings. When he got to us he said to Dad, "Mr Panton?" Father said, "Yes?" "I'm Christian Nielsen, your son's pilot." He had just come back from a German prisoner of war camp. He was Canadian and he had come from Bournemouth, because the ministry had sent him to explain to my father what had happened to them on the night that they were shot down and that was quite a surprise. So my father took him home to talk to him, while I stayed to carry on digging the garden and now, as I look back, I just cannot believe that I didn't go home with him.

So, when they got home, Nielsen told my father, that on the night they were shot down, they were on their way to Nuremberg, flying at 20,000 ft. They were getting ready for their bomb run, the bomb aimer was getting set up to offload and they were around forty miles from Nuremberg. It was a bright, moonlit night and there had been a hard frost over the city. He said that you could see all the streets shining like pieces of ribbon, about the width of your finger, with all the moonlight reflecting off the frost, even in the blackout. Nielsen told Father that at that point, Chris said, "Starboard inner engine on fire, Skipper." Nielsen said that they tried to put the fire out using fire extinguishers, which were fitted around the engine, but it was to no avail. The flames from the fire swept right past the rear turret of the Halifax, so Chris Nielsen warned the crew he was going to go into a steep dive for 5000 ft to try and flush it out. But this didn't do the trick either and it took both Nielsen and his bomb aimer at the joystick to pull it out of its dive. Now, as I've already said, they had an extra pilot with them that night, one who was with them for experience, before he started his tour of operations. So when they managed to pull out of the dive, Nielsen told this second pilot to "Feather the engine," of the engine on fire, but the training pilot accidentally feathered the good engine, causing them to lose power on one side and at this stage they still had all their bombs on board. When they lost power on the wrong engine, Nielsen couldn't hold it and they descended into an uncontrollable dive, so he told the aircrew to abandon the aircraft swiftly. And those were the last words he ever spoke to any of the crew again. He reckoned they had no more than seven seconds to get out of the Halifax before it exploded in mid-air. Nielsen was blown out of the side of the aircraft, and he said that he had no idea how his parachute opened, but it did and he found himself landing in a little village on a square of grass. The rear gunner and the wireless operator got out and the rest were all killed.

Nielsen told Father that what had happened was a German night fighter had come up from underneath them where Chris's crew couldn't see it and set the inner engine on fire by shooting at them. He then came back again and hit the empty petrol tank, which is the most vital part of any aircraft to be hit. This is because an empty petrol tank with a bullet in blows up immediately; had it been a full tank it wouldn't have happened. After relaying the night's events to my father, Chris Nielsen then had to go back to Bournemouth to meet the crew, ready to go back to Canada, to Winnipeg. Nielsen sent a Christmas card to my Parents for two years after the War, but after that we never heard anything from him again.

Chapter Nine

The Dawn of Panton Bros Poultry Begins!

In April 1949, we were still catching rabbits and one day that spring, Father and I went to shoot some wood pigeons off a field of newly drilled peas, at a place called Grebby, near Spilsby, for a man called Mr Carl Rigaul. In 1949 you only had to shoot thirty pigeons to get a full day's pay, so Father and I had gone this particular day to keep the pigeons off the field of peas. We stopped shooting around 5 o'clock at night and decided to go home to Partney which was about three miles away. We had got a Ford 8 car at this stage and I was driving, because I was now seventeen. We had just come into Partney village when my Father said to me, "I want to stop at the telephone box, Fred; I've maybe bought a little smallholding." I said, "What's a smallholding?" because I'd never heard of one and when he got out of the car and went to the telephone box, I thought to myself, "I hope not!" I could see him dialling, then using the telephone and he came running back and got into the car and he said to me, "Aye Fred, I have got it!"

So what happened was, he hadn't told me, but a small farm had come up for sale at Stickford, which was about ten miles from Partney. He had bought nine acres of land, a house (which was very small – only two up and two down), a barn and a crew yard for beast. I was quite upset at that stage when he told me what he'd given for it. (He'd paid £1120.) He'd got a man to bid at a sale for him because he'd never bid at one before and he knew that I wanted to go into poultry farming. The reason I was upset was because he'd spent every penny we'd got at the time and we still had to go out to work to earn a living. This was on the Friday and I thought to myself, "I'll go and have a look at it this weekend."

This little farm was at Stickford, at the foot of the Lincolnshire Wolds, on the Lincolnshire Fens (which is flat land), which was strange after we'd been used to the hills. I had a motorbike at the time, a BSA 250, and on the Sunday morning I went to have a look. It was a dull and rainy day and I remember looking at the soil; it was black Fen soil, and when I got there I thought, "What a terrible place this is." I couldn't fancy myself living there, it was so dull and wet and it was flat and there were no trees. I remember that I was wearing a big, old, khaki army top coat and on the way home I thought I would just cut across to East Kirkby, which was only two miles away. The airfield by now was closed and there were no aircraft left there, so I made my way to the main runway where I used to watch the Lancasters taking off. I thought I might just see how fast this BSA250 would go on the runway and I got myself laid down over the handlebars in a fairly strong head wind and I made it to 75 mph, and that was absolutely flat out. I went home through Old Bolingbroke, back to Partney, still thinking of what a terrible place it looked at Stickford. I couldn't imagine myself living there, but we did. So that was on the 6th April that we bought it and we were able to flit there on the 12th April. It turned out to be the best day's work my father ever did, buying that farm. We had four acres of grass and five acres of arable land, on which I could start my poultry farming. So I would like to leave it at this point, for now, I shall be coming back to it later.

I mentioned that we had a Ford 8 car in 1949. Well, just before we left Old Bolingbroke to live at Partney Watermill, we bought the Ford 8 car from a Mr Walter Dennet, who my Father worked for. We needed it for us to go rabbiting in once I had left school. My Father bought this car, which was a 1933 model, for £30. Originally, he had wanted a motorbike and sidecar for us to go rabbiting together, but I remember saying to him, "I am *not* going out with you in a *side*car! It's a car or *nothing*." So we bought the Ford 8! Now, this car had been standing in its shed from the beginning till the end of the war and it had never been started up or run for five full years. So, about a week before we were about to leave to live at Partney, Mr Walter Dennet said to my Father, "We'll see if we can get this Ford 8 started for you now, Edward."

I remember it was a very rainy day, but Mr Dennet looked at the distributor, the brakes, checked the oil, the carburettor and fitted a new battery and new plugs; the whole works! Then he put a two gallon tin of petrol in the tank to see if it would start. With us living on a hill just above Old Bolingbroke, all we had to do was push the car out onto the road and let it freewheel down this hill in gear and let the clutch out. To our relief it did start and when we let the clutch out we carried on and turned round in Old Bolingbroke and drove it back up the hill, into the grass fields, so that Father could get used to handling the car. He had never driven a car before and he was having difficulty changing gear; stalling it and making it jump because he hadn't let the clutch out properly! It was quite a while before he could really master it.

As time went on, I found myself always cleaning and polishing the car and I kept it in nice condition. I thought quite a lot of that Ford 8, but after a time, I saw another Ford 8; a 1937 model and it looked to be in much nicer condition than ours. So I said to Dad that we ought to try and sell our Ford 8 and find out if this man would sell his 1937 model to us. The man said that he was prepared to, but he wanted £115 for it, and this seemed like quite a lot of money in those days.

This was all quite a while before we bought the little smallholding at Stickford. I had set my mind on it that I wanted to get this 1937 Ford 8 model, but in order to get it we had to sell our car first, so we decided we would take it to Boston market and put it on the stones to see if it would sell in the market place. Father took it and we got £100 for it, meaning we had made a profit of £70 on our original buying price. When he came home from the market, I was out at the time, and he was waiting for me in his chair. And when I arrived home and saw him sitting there in his chair by the fire I said to him, "Did you get the car sold?" He told me yes, and I asked him how much he made for it, and when he told me £100. I said, "It didn't!" and he told me the auctioneers paid him for it in pound notes. He showed me he had this £100, in notes in his hands, holding it ready to show me. It makes me emotional to remember what he said to me here; "I shall never forget, Fred, that this is the first time that I have ever held one hundred pounds in my hands, in my life." We did buy the other, 1937, car, for £115.

Just going back to my football days at Partney, the pick of the league played the Lincoln City Colts team at the Skegness Town football ground. One week after we'd bought the smallholding at Stickford, I was playing centre-forward, and that day, which was a Saturday, I happened to score a hat trick against the Lincoln City Colts team. On the Monday, I received a letter from Mr Anderson, who was the Lincoln City football manager, asking me to go for a trial. I went for the trial and I was accepted onto the Colts team. During the trial Mr Anderson was playing centre-half against me, but I never managed to score any goals through him! But I was accepted and I used to go twice a week for training and the reason for which I am giving you this story is because if I had received that letter one week earlier, my father would never have bought our little smallholding at Stickford.

So we moved to Stickford to the little farm that Father bought on the 6th April 1949. We had four acres of grass land and five acres of ploughed land, so after arriving at Stickford and starting our journey in poultry farming, the first thing my Father did was buy twenty eight chickens and put them in the crew yard. We then started building small poultry houses; about 10 ft wide and 12 ft long. We bought one hundred and fifty, day-old baby chicks and we would rear them from day-old to the point of lay. We bought these day-old chicks, which were a Rhode Island Red / Black Leghorn cross, from Mr Drakes of Horncastle. So we were building these huts and also having to go out catching rabbits whilst we reared enough poultry to enable us to stay at home permanently. For the first two years we continued building poultry houses and buying more day-old baby chicks. Within those two years, we had built up to three hundred and fifty chickens. I remember when we got the first 150 pullets fully reared up to laying condition; in the first poultry house we had one hundred and thirteen poultry and some days we used to get one hundred and thirteen eggs! Every bird had laid which sometimes I could hardly believe.

We carried on with building up our poultry and going rabbit catching for our weekly money to live on, while we were developing the business, and I would have been eighteen years of age by this point. My youngest brother, Harold, had been finished from school for quite a bit now and he would be coming into the business, but he couldn't start immediately until we got ourselves more established. So he had to go and work on a neighbouring farm until such a time came he could join us, although he did help us in any spare time that he wasn't working on the other farm. In 1951 Harold turned eighteen and he was called for National Service for two years. He was a signal man for the Captain, which means that he would ride in the Jeep with the Captain. He was based in Goslar in Germany and he ended up being a Lance Corporal. The reason I didn't have to do my National Service was because I was working on the land, so I was deferred. So after he had been in the army for two years, he came home during 1953. By this point we had got the business built up enough for Harold to stay and come into the business, so we started our partnership together. We have been business partners now for sixty one years and as far as I'm concerned, this has turned out to be a very successful partnership.

I would like to say here that after leaving school I did not take a wage from the business for ten years, I asked for nothing, otherwise we would not have been able to become established. In fact, I never took a wage until I got married in 1956, and even then I only took £5 per week! It was the same for Harold when he married in 1958, and he also only took £5 per week. As we were continuing with poultry and developing the business, we were in a position to start farming a few pigs as well. We were only building small poultry houses, until one day, when Father and I were on our way to a place called Hareby, on the other side of East Kirkby airfield, we drove across the old airfield and saw some men taking down the living quarters, the billets. They were just knocking them down and taking them away on lorries, so I said to my father, "I think we ought to stop, there's no need to be knocking those buildings down. We should go and ask them if we can have one or two of them to use as poultry houses. We can soon take them down." So we stopped and asked these men if it was possible to have one of these buildings for a poultry hut. The billets were 60ft long and 20ft wide, which at that time looked very long buildings to us; just the buildings we needed to keep chickens! However, when we asked the men, they said, "We can't give you permission, but we'll give you the address that you can write to." The address was for the Ministry of Works, so my father wrote a letter to them, explaining who we were and what we wanted and that we were interested in buying one of the buildings for poultry use. When the letter came back, it said that if we were interested, they would sell us all the buildings. There was a mix of three types and sizes of buildings; the Nissan huts, Lang huts and Jane huts, which were 60ft by 20ft. They offered the price of £18 for the larger ones, and £12 for the Nissan huts, but all we were able to afford at the time, was one large hut, which we did buy. So we took it down from the airfield and put it up on our farm for our chickens and after this, all of our neighbouring farms also wanted one, so I had the job of buying these sheds from the ministry for our local farmers. This also meant that I had to take them down and build them up again, earning a little bit of money. Some farmers would buy two of these houses, occasionally even three and this used to upset me to a certain degree, to think that we could only afford to buy one. However, this turned out to be a good thing in the end, because the Lang type of building on the airfield started coming up for sale after a time and they were made of a much better material. They had a better roof, with asbestos and they lasted longer in comparison to the Jane hut, which was made from black tin. So we finished up with 11 of these buildings in our little grass paddock for poultry. In fact, it finished looking like the billets of an army camp!

At this time, the Ministry of Works was in charge of dismantling all the ex-war aircraft; Halifax, Lancasters, Wellington, Beaufort and so on, taking them to pieces so that all the different makes could be melted down for the aluminium. By now, we were very well established with the ministry of works; we knew them and they knew us very well. As you now know, my brother was on aircrew flying Halifax bombers when he was killed and I often used to think about Chris, even though this was about five to six years after the war. One day, I suddenly thought that I would say to my Father that I should like to see if it was possible to get a Halifax bomber (the same kind of plane that Chris used to fly in) which we could stand in our farm yard. So I said to my father, "I reckon we ought to see if we can get a Halifax bomber. They're going at £100 a piece." You could have your pick from either a new one or one that had done its tour of operations and I wanted one out of respect for my brother. My Father, however, wouldn't hear of it and said to me, "You are *not* having one of those things here."

In 1949, when we moved to Stickford, I wanted to travel to Germany to find where Chris had crashed and go to look at his grave, but again, Father would not hear of it. He simply did not want me to go. I kept asking, but was just told that "You needn't bother to go." He just didn't want it. The same was true of my intentions for the Halifax bomber; I would keep asking and he just carried on refusing. So one night, I thought to myself, "I'll just ask him once more" and I remember very well that it was a lovely summer's night. It had been a hot day and my father had been pumping a bucket of water because we had some baby ducks and they wanted a drink. So I went up to him pumping this water, just to have another go at him about the Halifax and when I asked him, he stopped pumping the water, looked me right in the eye and said, " If I've told you once, I've told you a hundred times. Now, I'm going to tell you once and for all, you are *not* having one of those *mucky* things here!"

I knew then that it was final and I never bothered thinking about it anymore. In fact, I lost all interest in the war and the war years; I just focused fully on my business.

Fred at Stickford Farm

Cutting wheat at Stickford, 1954, with Fred on the binder;
Bill Spinks on the Tractor

Fred's first chickens

Chickens leaving Stickford farm

Chapter Ten

She's The One

The time came when I was going to Lincoln twice a week for training. Father and I would be planning out our work and Dad would come up with what we had to do, but I would say "Well I can't, I'm at Lincoln tomorrow", and this was starting to happen quite frequently because important jobs were falling on the days when I needed to be at my training. So one day Father said to me, "Now Fred, you're going to have to make your mind up soon. Do you want to do your footballing or do you want your farming?" because it was starting to get in the way of work, with needing to go to Lincoln and back all the time. So I thought about it, and I came to the conclusion that football might last for ten or twenty years, but farming would last a lifetime. So I decided that I would call it the end of the day for football, which wasn't one of the nicest decisions I've ever had to make, but I knew it was the right thing to do; and that was that. These were the years in the mid-1950s; roughly around 1954. We were beginning to get ourselves nicely established with our chickens and our few pigs; so much so that we now didn't have to go out rabbit catching so much. This was a very good thing because the disease myxomatosis had broken out in our area, which put a stop to rabbit catching for us, so thus began the end of one era and started another.

So we kept expanding in different parts with pigs and chickens, and I remember one day, we were putting another building up for pigs. For our poultry we used to use Spillers Food from Grimsby, but a BOCM food representative used to visit to see if we would like to use BOCM foods for our pigs. This man used to call and see us once a fortnight, but we never changed, we carried on using Spillers, and this BOCM chap often used to say to me, whilst we were building a new piggery, "You used to have a brother flying during the war?" and I would say "Yes, I did", but I never used to stop working, because I had lost interest in the war now, but he would say to me "I was aircrew too." He flew with 617 squadron from RAF Scampton, and he happened to be one of the men on the Dambuster raid with Guy Gibson. But all I would reply back was "Oh, yes?" and would never enlarge on anything. Fifty years on, however, I wish that I had spoken to him. You see, these meetings usually never happen by chance, I've found, and I remember that quite well. After a time we were in a position buy more bits of land, and start renting other parts, here and there, in order to enlarge the business. I remember when we were building poultry units in the grass field and we had them scattered all round. It eventually got to the point when we needed a tractor and trailer to take food and water round, because it was becoming too big a job to do by hand. We had a little Ford Standard tractor, but we didn't have a trailer to put behind it and we couldn't really afford to buy one, so we were finding it a bit difficult. One day, I went to help our neighbouring farmer to pick potatoes and my father came to see me in the field and said to me, "Fred, the only way that we can afford a trailer is to sell the car." This was our green 1937 Ford 8 model in showroom condition and I'd kept it absolutely immaculate, almost as new. Before he said this, we had been offered a tip-up trailer for £80, and even though it was one of the older trailers that you had to pump by hand, we knew that it was just what we needed. Father said that there was a farmer who was interested in buying our Ford 8 car for £400 and he had a Ford 8 van of his own which he was selling for £220, which meant that we could take that and also buy the trailer for £80 and still have £100 over! So I agreed with my father that we should sell our car for the van and trailer, but it grieved me, really, to do it. This was back in 1952 and we have still got this trailer in one of our buildings, making it sixty years ago since we bought it. I have since told my two lads, "Never, ever, sell that trailer; we had to sell our very best car to buy it, so it still means a lot to me."

This particular year, around autumn of 1952, I was going on the standard Ford tractor one day to do some work with it on one of our fields, which we had just bought. This was nearly a mile away from where we lived and on my way to this field, I could see this girl picking potatoes. She was about a hundred metres from the road, as she stood there in the middle of this twenty acre field, which was a large field in those days. She was by herself, all alone, and she was doing one of the worst jobs you can do on a farm, which is going back and picking all the harrowings, which are the small potatoes that had been missed in the first instance. It's back-aching, hard work bending over all day, picking up potatoes and this girl was out there in this field, on her own every day for a month. She picked them into a basket before she put them in bags, which were scattered all over the field. Now, I had to go past this field quite a few times during this spring; backwards and forwards on the tractor and I thought to myself "If she can do that job day in and day out, on her own, then that's the girl I'm looking for to be my wife." So I got to know her name was Betty and where she lived and I started waving to her, putting my hand up while she was in the field and she'd put her hand up, back. As well as this, my friend, Derek Hipkin, and I used to go running together and on our route we used to run past Betty's house, which was only a mile from my own house. I would make sure that I timed it for six o'clock every time we went, which was always a Monday night, which happened to be wash day for Betty, so I knew that she would be in her house, standing near her window, ironing. So as we past her house, I would just hang back a little from Derek and fall back maybe a step or two, so that he was just in front of me, then I would look back and wave at her. And I would never let Derek see me do this! I found out years later that Betty would always be there by the window on purpose, hoping that I would be running past!

I'd never been out with a girl in my life; she was the first girl ever to attract me. So I did a little bit more detective work, finding out who she was, where she came from, etc, and the jigsaw all started coming together for me. It seemed to me that she was just the girl that I was looking for. I found out that she was a farmer's daughter, a Sunday school teacher and she was a Methodist, as were my father and I.

I also found out that her name was Betty Clement and at this time, in 1952, she was twenty three years of age. She worked and lived at home with her parents and she helped her father with different jobs on the farm and, of course, this just made me even keener and more interested! Betty was one of three of Mr Clement's daughters and was the middle child. She had an elder sister called Joan and a younger sister called Judy. My father and her father, Mr Clement, knew each other and were good friends. Mr Clement had around one hundred acres of arable farm land, a mile away from us and he employed three or four people on his farm. So it was all beginning to fit the bill! Seeing her on her own, working in the field and finding out that she was a Sunday school teacher; the more I found out about her, I didn't need any more references. I knew that I wanted her, that she was the one for me. The problem was that she already had a boyfriend and so, in order to get nearer to her, I started to go to Stickford Chapel in the village. I didn't actually find out what her name was until I started going to her chapel to get to know her!

She was so smart and lovely looking and so sensible, I just knew that she was going to be the one for me, but I had this problem! And I thought that there was no way I'd be able to have her because of this other man. I used to watch her coming out of Church every Sunday with her boyfriend, walking past my house, arm in arm, and it was difficult, because this was the girl that I knew I wanted to marry! I used to think to myself, "How am I ever going to run off a trainee minister from the scene?" I was so desperate to get her. Now, I know that it seems so selfish of me to think of her like that, but I was head-over-heels in love with her. I used to pray to the Lord every day, "If I can only have her, I will look after her for the rest of my life, I want to marry her." I would take my parents with me to Chapel, which, of course, suited them just fine. I think that they had an inkling that it was because I was keen on a girl, but they never said anything. I think my father smelled a rat, but he never let on!

When I started seeing her at Chapel every Sunday, I was already head over heels for her, but I was so nervous that I hardly dared to speak to her, just to say hello. After a little while she came up to me at the end of the service and told me that there were some mice in the church and asked if I could come and set up some traps for her. Well, of course, that was exactly what I wanted to hear! So I went with her and set the traps for her and we would be talking and getting to know one another. This started to become a regular occurrence as she would come to me at the end of Sunday services and tell me that she thought there were some more mice again, so could I come and set some more traps for her? As you can imagine, this was no problem for me so I was very happy to do this for her and spend more time with her. Mr Clement knew Dad and they started talking at the Sunday Chapel services and would sometimes invite us back for a cup of tea after the service. Of course, I would always go because I wanted to see Betty! After a while she asked me if I wanted to go to the youth club, which was every Saturday night at the Methodist Chapel and of course I jumped at the idea! So the arrangement was that I used to pick her up in our van, which was the van we used for everything on the farm. So I always cleaned it out every week before I picked her up. We would then go and pick up four or five more young people on the way, and we had to be home by 10 o'clock at the latest. For several months I never got the chance to ask her if she would go out with me, but the more I met her, the keener I was. Eventually, I found out that her boy friend had left her. He'd gone and they'd broken up. Betty had never told me this, somebody else told me. So after a while I decided to take a different route home from the youth club. I planned it so that she was the last one to be dropped off so that I could get her on her own to ask her out! This little plan worked and I did ask her if she would go out with me; she could hardly believe that I'd asked her! But the answer that I got wasn't the answer that I wanted… she said to me, "I'll think about it; I want a fortnight to think about it." I couldn't believe it! That fortnight seemed like fourteen years! But at the end of that fortnight, she said "We'll give it a try, but just as friends for the time being," and I thought, "Well that's half the answer!" So we started going out as friends, but after a time of being together, it was clear how we felt about each other and we've never looked back.

One evening, after Betty and I had been courting for a little time, I had run over to Derek's house to meet him for our weekly run. I was in the yard waiting for him to get his running shoes on and Mrs Hipkin was leaning against the door when she said to me, "Is it right that you're seeing Betty Clement, Fred?" and I said proudly, "Yes I am, Mrs Hipkin." She smiled broadly and said to me, "Well you've got a very nice girl there, Fred." I blushed and simply replied, "Yes I have Mrs Hipkin. I know, thank you very much."

Betty was the only girl I ever looked at all my life. There was never anybody else, it was always her. It took me two years in total to get her, but I knew that I wanted her for my wife all of that time.

Betty with her parents and sister Judy

Betty as a young woman

Fred and Betty – getting to know you

Chapter Eleven

A Tight Deadline and a Midnight Mission.

In 1953, we lived seventeen miles from Skegness and I can remember very well when the East Coast floods came; it was one of the worst storms and roughest nights that I've ever known. I'm mentioning this because my father and I used to catch moles on the golf course at Sutton-On-Sea and the great storms of 1953 brought the tide over and destroyed this golf course, as well as the pier at Skegness and many people lost their lives. The storm damaged some of our poultry house roofs, but nothing compared to what it did on the East Coast.

As time went on, we were carrying on expanding our poultry business and I'd just like to tell you about some of the ex-RAF buildings that we bought. Two of these RAF buildings we bought from a place called Skellingthorpe, near Lincoln, and these were known as the 'Lang' type of building, which were built by Lang's building contractors. We found out later, once we'd bought them and they'd been delivered, that some of the Dambuster crews had been billeted in these buildings during the war, just before they had gone on the Dambuster raid, which I was surprised and very pleased about; to think that we had two of the original buildings that the Dambuster crew lived in! There was also another building that we had bought from out Derbyshire way which was going to be delivered on a set date to the farm by a Mr Hopwell, who lived at Sandyacre at Nottingham. This would have been around 1955, as I recall. The building, which was 70 feet long by 20 feet wide, was due to be delivered three weeks after we had purchased it, so whilst we were waiting, Harold and I built the foundations and got it cemented ready for the delivery. The baby chicks, pure Rhode Island Reds, had already been ordered from Mr Drakers of Horncastle, ready to be delivered four weeks from the day we purchased the building. So the building was going to have to be delivered by the second week of October, in time for our chick delivery. However, bad weather started to set in with rain, wind and short days and it got to the 20th October, and the building still hadn't been delivered. They were having difficulty in taking the buildings down because of the weather and I knew very well that the baby chicks were due to be delivered on the 6th November. We reached the 30th October and our building still hadn't been delivered, so my brother,

Father and I were starting to get very anxious. The chicks were in their incubators, so they couldn't be cancelled and we wouldn't cancel them anyway, because of the time factor. So, when it got to the 4th November and the building still hadn't arrived, we only had forty eight hours before the chicks were due to be delivered and we didn't have a hut to put them in! We were getting very nervous and hot under the collar! After many heated telephone calls to Mr Hopwell, it turned out that it would be impossible to bring the building before the 5th November because of all the bad weather. When it did eventually arrive, having travelled all the way from Derbyshire, it was five minutes past midnight. Now, this will take some believing, but it's all true. So there was my brother and I and another hard working lad whose name was Monty Thompson. We'd already been working all day and we drew up a plan that when our building was delivered, we would take it off the lorry, onto three other trailers to take it down to the field where Harold and I had set the foundations. By now we knew that we would have to work all through the night.

It was a very foggy night and the lorry driver had had to drive through thick fog all the way from Derbyshire to Stickford, which was a seventy or eighty mile single way trip. But when the delivery did arrive, Father gave him a good breed for arriving so late! He shouted out of his bedroom window, across the yard to him in his lorry and the driver was so upset at this, he said, "Well if I had known this was going to happen, then I shouldn't have bothered driving all this distance, just so I could get a telling off!" Dad was that mad at him that I had to cool things down a bit! So after we had spoken to the lorry driver and taken him a cup of tea before he went back, you can imagine once he had gone, that you could've cut the atmosphere with a knife!

Now, we didn't have electricity on the farm in those days, so we had to space six tilley lamps all around the footings to illuminate the area in which we were going to be working. We started to put the building up at 1 o'clock in the morning and had to work very, very hard that night. We parted the end section and then the side section to hold the corner together and I want to say now, that of all the poultry buildings we'd ever put up in daylight, we'd never had a poultry hut go up so quickly and so well, with no snags, as this hut did. Every part fitted like a glove; all the pieces bolted and slotted together perfectly, and at half past seven in the morning precisely, I was just nailing the last sheet of asbestos to the roof of the building as the daylight began to break…and the baby chicks were due to be delivered at 10 o'clock! After we had finished putting the building together we still had to fit a Calor gas brooder in the roof to keep the chicks warm, which meant we had to connect all the piping and the gas bottles to produce the gas heat for the baby chicks. We had to have the temperature in the building at 89'C to keep the chicks warm, but with the building being so big (70ft long by 20ft wide) to get this kind of temperature we had to put in two stack sheets to section the building, which let us get the temperature up quickly, keeping it all in one area. On the floor, we put felt down first, to stop the damp and cold from coming up, then we covered this with lots of wood shavings, to keep the chicks warm. We could then get the water fountains working for the chick troughs, and you know, we never stopped working for a drink or anything, from when the building was delivered to when we completed the job, just before 9 o'clock in the morning.

The baby chicks came at 11 o'clock in the morning and those chicks did so well. In fact, I think they did the best of any chickens that we've ever had! After we'd got all that ready, we then had to go round all the rest of the poultry to check and feed them. After we'd been round all the other birds, we stopped to have our breakfast and after we'd had something to eat we went back to our baby chicks to check that they were all right and warm. We'd only just finished everything by 2 o'clock in the afternoon. I shall never forget, because Harold, Monty and me were all sitting on the side of the four-wheeled trailer having a rest and Monty sat in the middle between Harold and me. I said to Monty, "We've done it Mont; I didn't think we could, but we have," and I said, "You know Mont, we worked all day yesterday, all through the night, until 2 o'clock this afternoon. It's amazing." Monty never answered me and when I turned my head to look at him, he'd gone to sleep! When he woke up and opened his eyes, I said to Mont, "I think we'll call it a day."

Even today, I find it hard to believe, but it's absolutely true and we never had to cancel those birds!

Betty and I were getting along very well and the business was acquiring more land whenever possible to continue growing. So life was moving forward nicely for us. By this point, it was autumn of 1954 and we had been together for a year. So I decided that the time had come. I took her out one night and I asked her to marry me and, of course, I was delighted when she accepted. We went together to choose her ring from Harvey Gills jewellers of Boston, and then we went home to surprise everybody with our news! I asked Mr Clement for his permission to marry his daughter, but I did this after Betty had already said yes, because I didn't want to risk her saying no to me after her Dad had said yes! Bett and I were thinking about where we were going to live when we got married and eventually, we reached the decision that we were going to build a little bungalow, or put up a pre-fabricated house on this little field that we owned, next to our farm. They were advertising pre-fabricated houses from London to be bought and delivered for £180. So we organised the local builder in the village, a man called Ray Newton, who we knew had put pre-fabs up before, so we gave him the job to erect the bungalow. The time came when our bungalow was finished and we fixed the wedding day for January 6th 1956. When the wedding day came it was very foggy, with freezing fog. We were married at Spilsby Methodist Chapel and I remember that it was a particularly slippery and frosty day and two people had accidents on their way to the wedding! So we got married and we held the reception in the schoolroom at Stickford Chapel.

After the wedding, we went to London on our honeymoon for one week – we had to be back by the following Monday because we had a lot of chicks coming into one of the poultry houses! While we were away on our honeymoon, there came a very bad snowstorm at home in Stickford which put the electricity off for a whole fortnight. There was so much snow that the flat-roofed bungalow gathered more than eighteen inches of it and Harold and father thought that the roof would cave in, so they both went to shovel it off, thinking that the roof wouldn't bear the weight of the snow. The farm, and the whole village, had no electricity, so they all had to use tilley lamps everywhere in order to do all the work.

So we arrived back from our honeymoon and we got settled into our little pre-fabricated bungalow. Harold had been with me for two years now, working together and had met and was now courting a young lady named Lucy Louth.

Now, when Mr Newton was building our little bungalow, he had a man helping him with the foundations called Mr Butler. He'd been talking to me one day, while we were building and he told me that he'd been in the Navy during the war and he had acquired a pair of German submarine binoculars. He asked me if I was interested in looking at them, because he was thinking about selling them and I told him that I would very much like to have a look at them and I asked him to bring them in. So he brought these binoculars in a leather case with the German Swastika stamp and he told me that he wanted £30 for them. Now, I must say that these were the best binoculars I have ever seen in my life! Just outside our little bungalow there was a very large grass field of sixty acres and one night, after tea, whilst it was still daylight, I decided to give the binoculars a really good test. Through them, I could see rabbits and hares, anything that was alive and moving, sitting on a tuft of grass or running around, at the end of this field, which I'd never have been able to see through an ordinary pair of binoculars. I could not believe how good they were. So I said to Betty, "Do you fancy a rabbit for Sunday dinner, or a hare?" because I still had my 2.2 rifle from my rabbiting days and I used to shoot rabbits and hares in this big grass field. The reason I'm telling you this story, is that whenever we wanted one for dinner, my wife would have these German binoculars, I would look first, just to find the rabbit which would be two hundred, maybe two hundred and fifty yards away, sometimes more, which showed up so clearly through these binoculars. So Bett would look through the lens to find the rabbit that I was going to try and shoot and we would stand in the bedroom with the window wide open. I would have my 2.2 rifle and I would set the sight up on the gun and Betty would look to see if I had gone over the top, or shot too short. She would tell me precisely where the bullet had landed, so that I could set my sight accurately as to where to shoot. She would say, "You've missed it, you were too short." So I would load another bullet in my rifle and shoot again and she would say "You've got it!" Then I would go out of the bungalow, across the field to pick it up and we would have it for our Sunday dinner. We did that quite often, but we couldn't have done it without these binoculars, they were so good. So, as I said, the man wanted £30 for them and £30 was a lot of money in those days, especially after we'd just got married and built this bungalow. So it was quite a while before I made my mind up, but at the same time Mr Butler had another man very interested in them, so he took them to let this other man have a look. This other man, unfortunately, bought them right away, so I had to give them up, but it was a bit too much, at the time for us to afford. I have regretted it ever since though, not buying them.

Fred's Growing Family and Expanding Farming Life

Chapter Twelve

Farms, Fathers, Brothers, Children, a few Chickens

And a squealing dog

We now have to jump forward two years to 1957. We were by now expecting our first child, Phillip, and Phillip was born on March 6th 1957, my birthday. I shall always remember that it was five minutes before 6 o'clock at night, and the weather forecast was just coming on when I received a telephone call and was asked to go to the Grace Swan Hospital in Hundleby, near Spilsby. We had a little son, who we named Phillip William Panton. I was so over the moon because he had been delivered on my birthday and because of the economics of it; it worked with my sense of humour that with us having a birthday on the same day, we could have the same cake!

I haven't mentioned yet, which I would like to, that when we came to Stickford in 1949, I became friendly with a lad called Derek Hipkin, and his brother Ray Hipkin. He was a very nice lad and we are still very good friends. I found out that Derek used to do a lot of long distance running and I had always been interested in long distance running myself. His brother, Ray, was very good at short distances of 100m and 220m. Derek and I started running about 16 miles on average twice every week after work until, eventually, we decided to take up our running professionally and we would go as far as Goole and Brough for our athletic running. We even became friendly with the Lincolnshire champion miler, Jim Ebdon, who would look after us and train us on a regular basis and we both did very well at our long distance running. We each had a motorbike back then, and mine was a 250 BSA and Derek had an Ariel motorcycle, and as I say, we were very close friends.

Before I met Betty, Derek and I found out that "Just Jane", who was the daily pin-up girl for the Daily Mirror paper during the wartime, was advertised in our local paper as coming to Skegness to give a show at one of the theatres. Although it was very rarely that we went out anywhere together, Derek and I decided that we would go and see her show, but my parents must never know and I dared not ever tell them and Derek was the same! So it was this particular Saturday night that we went and as we came out from the show and were walking over to our motorbikes to come home, because it was a very cold night, I was just putting this very big khaki top coat on and fastening the buttons, when I said to Derek, "If I ever get married and have a daughter, I'm going to call her Jane." At the same time, I used to think that I should love to have twin girls; I had seen two twin girls together and I remember thinking how beautiful they looked. It was amazing to me to see two people, exactly the same. There is nothing prettier on this Earth than identical twin girls, to me.

When we arrived home that night from seeing "Just Jane", I was fifteen minutes late home, I should have been home at 10 o'clock at the latest and when I arrived home it was quarter past. Father, Mother and Harold had gone to bed, so when I came to the house I had to unlock the door quietly and go upstairs as silently as possible so that nobody could hear me. That went well, but the next morning, the first thing that Father said to me was, "You were late home last night, where had you been?" I stalled and said "I didn't think I was that late!" and he looked at me and said, "You were because I heard you come home!" and then he said more firmly, "Don't you ever let that happen again," and I knew that he meant it. He said to me, "I was looking out the bedroom window, listening and waiting for you and I don't want to ever have to do that again." He was worried about me. I got over that anyway, but I have thought about it a lot since, years later, how we actually plucked up the courage to get the nerve to go!

Now, back to Phillip, who was born in 1957. Betty and I were then to expect our second child for February of 1960. So Bett was pregnant and it got to three months before the birth, when we found out that we were going to have twins! Our doctor said to my wife, "How's the knitting going?" My good wife looked surprised and asked, "Why, how many are in there?" and he told her that she wasn't just having one, but there were two babies! So when we got over the surprise and shock, I was very pleased, because I was hoping and praying that I would get my identical twin girls! This, however, wasn't meant to be. I think that someone knew better than me! When they were born it turned out that we'd got a baby girl and a little baby boy. We had two beautiful, healthy baby twins. So I called the girl Jane, like I said I would, Jane Eva, and we called the boy David Royce Panton. So Betty, after they were born, was kept very busy!

We had our three children, Phillip and the twins. In the night, when they needed to be fed, I had Jane and Betty would always have David and after hoping for two girls, I've come to realise since they have both grown up and

David and Phillip are in the business, carrying on the poultry, that the Lord knew better than I did. It turns out that he knew that I had to have another son to carry on the business. I've come to realise this more and more, at this age of eighty one, that that was the best thing that could have happened, to be blessed with a twin boy and girl. Although I say this, Phillip is a very nice lad; very quiet, he thinks deeply and has the patience of Job, and he's very good at all the figures and the paper work; whereas David is very much like myself. Phillip, in fact, reminds me a lot of Harold, with his personality, strengths and traits. But David, I can see is very, very much like me; full of go, organising and building everything, very capable. They are both capable of running the businesses and, although I am still very active in my work, I am confident that I can leave them to it and they will do me proud.

So we'll return again to 1959, to Harold and Lucy Louth, who had now married. In 1958, we had built them another pre-fabricated bungalow, next to ours. Harold had his first born, a son he named Paul, born in June 1960, then a daughter, Linda, around 1963. Then came another daughter, Frances, born around 1966. Harold's son, Paul, came into the business on finishing school.

Something, which is very important to me to talk about, regards my late father-in-law, Mr Clement. He decided that he wanted to retire from arable farming, which he had done all his life and wanted instead to go into poultry farming, like us. So he had a sale of all of his implements and stock and spent the rest of his life growing chickens, just for a pastime to keep his mind busy. I had the job of helping him put some poultry houses up, just enough to keep him busy and occupied with farming his land. I helped him quite a lot until we got him established as he only lived about one mile away from where we lived. Although it's me that says it, my father-in law was a very fine man. He was a Methodist lay preacher all his grown life and I never knew him any different in his temperament, he never altered. I respected him to such a degree because of how he used to work so hard all his life, from my first knowing him up to when he died, that I always addressed him as Mr Clement to his face, I couldn't bring myself to call him Father or Dad. So about a year before he died, my wife went up to see her father and when she arrived, he was sitting in his chair in his house and he said to Bett, "Before anything happens to me, Fred has never, ever, called me Pop or Dad and I should love to hear him call me Dad." My wife came home and told me what he had said and I was so touched by that that I said to her, "Yes Bett, I'll try, I will do some time," but when it came to it, I just couldn't do it. I respected him to such a degree, that it seemed to me to degrade him to call him Pop. Mr Clement was a man for whom I possessed the greatest respect; he was a marvellous man. He always practised what he preached and I never heard him raise his voice in all the years that I knew him.

To give you some idea, I must just tell you this little story. One night, my good friend and neighbour, Freddy Johnson and I went in his car to see my father-in-law. We drove into his farmyard and were talking to Mr Clement for a while, before we decided to come back home. Mr Clement had a black and white dog and when we were ready to set off, this dog was running around us and fussing. Freddy started the car, but as he drove forward, the car stalled and ran backwards onto the dog's tail. The dog was yelping, squealing and pulling, in terrible pain and Mr Clement gently put his head through the window, motioned his hand backwards and said, "Just reverse a little Freddy, you're on the old dog's tail." Freddy and I just couldn't believe how cool, calm and collected Mr Clement was, as he just waved his hand gently to motion the car to reverse to relieve this poor dog, who was barking and twisting and making all this noise!

Mr Clement was so calm and non-excitable, it was amazing. Freddy Johnson never forgot that; he reminded me for years and years afterwards that he'd never seen a man so cool. My father-in-law was a very fine man and I can't speak highly enough of him. On one occasion, I recall, when I first started seeing Betty, I was talking to him one night, sitting on a chair in his house about the Planet Earth and how it had come to be. I shall always remember that he said to me, "Fred, whenever you're driving down the road and you see a pile of stones, you know for *certain* that somebody put them there. It's the same with our Earth; somebody put it here, and that somebody was God." I've always thought that was a beautiful way to look at it.

So, now I'll take you to the 1960s when we were being kept busy with our farming stock. In 1962, a little farm came up to let, with one hundred and nineteen acres of land. I thought that it would be all right for us, if we could get it for putting the poultry manure onto. So we made an application and Father and I went for an interview to Lincoln to the land agents; Jas Martin & Co. who let the land. The farm belonged to Amcotts and we were successful in getting the tenancy for it. Once we had got the extra land, which was a lot in 1962, Harold and I discussed how we would manage this new purchase. We eventually thought that we would ask our elder brother, Roland, if he wanted to move into the farmhouse and be responsible for the land and we also kept another man who already lived and worked on the farm to stay and work with us. So we went to see Roly one night to see if he would be interested and he said that he was sure he would, but he would have to think about it for a while. Roly had been working on a dairy farm for nearly 30 years, since he left school and his interests were very much into cows and milking and I knew it would be a hard decision for him. Now, Roland was up in the hills in the Lincolnshire Wolds, which is very pretty, whereas we were based on the Lincolnshire Fen flat land, so it was very different scenery from what he was used to. After a time of thinking, he decided it was a kind and good offer, so he said that he would come and try it, which Harold and I were very pleased about. So Roly gave his notice in and he came to us at Fen Farm, Stickford, late on April 6th, Lady Day. During his time working on Fen Farm he truly enjoyed it, but at the same time he also missed his cows. He loved his dairy farming and after three years, very reluctantly, he wanted to go back to his milk cows. Roland was a very hard worker; he worked all his life from 4 o'clock in the morning until 8-9 o'clock at night, which he also did on our land, but in the end he had to go back to cattle and, of course, we understood his position, and agreed he should go back to his beloved vocation. The hills drew him back, if you like, from the flat land of the fen! But he always came to see us, nearly every week and he's now retired at over 90 years of age, in very good health and, you know he still comes over to see me every week. I have a lovely little story about my brother Roly. Ever since he was twelve years old, he has chained smoked all of his life, and it became very characteristic of Roly to have a cigarette constantly in his mouth! But one day, during his eighties he went to see the doctor with a bit of a cough, which turned out to be a chest infection. The doctors advised him to give up smoking and you know, from that day on, he quit, just like that. He just gave up and has never had another cigarette since. There's not many people who have been chain smoking all their lives who can just one day, all of a sudden, stop smoking as easily as Roly did and never have another one again!

So we were now left with an empty farmhouse and Harold and I decided it was best that he left his pre-fabricated bungalow to go and live at Fen Farm to look after our arable land, and I would continue to look after the poultry. Harold would come and help out with the chickens when we needed him, which he did a lot, in fact. Harold became nicely settled at Fen Farm and we were now growing sugar beet, potatoes, spring and winter barley, wheat and vegetables. In 1963, we started growing potatoes on a contract for Smith's crisps, a type called Record potatoes, which I liked very much because they were a nice, round shape. We were growing these for several years and we expanded our field for these up to fifty acres, on their own.

Going back to the arable farming, up until 1956, we used to bind all our corn and then stook it with a tractor and binder from 1949 up to 1956, until we decided to start using combines, which we have used ever since. The last year that we used a tractor and binder we had thirteen corn stacks, which we had to thrash with the old thrashing drum and then we completely changed to go with combine harvesters, which, of course, made combining a lot easier. As for our poultry, we had quite a large turnaround of commercial egg production, both free range and intensive. During 1950 - 1960, we decided to go in for breeding poultry, supplying hatching eggs to a firm called Thornber's at Mytholmroyd, in Yorkshire's Calder Valley. The parent stock we had in the late 50s was for the 505 and the 606, which were the first two breeds that we had. We found that it worked out more profitable to supply hatching eggs than commercial egg production. With having these quite big poultry houses, the ex RAF buildings from the airfields, we were getting so that we were keeping the birds more intensively than free range. When we made enquiries to Thornber's to see if we could start supplying hatching eggs, they were very interested and they duly sent John Dove, a representative, to come and see us. They were very pleased that we had made enquiries because they wanted to get established in this part of Lincolnshire with breeding. The only one thing that they were concerned about on our farm was that we were going more over to an intensive rearing system. The representative told us that the only thing which could stop us from supplying hatching eggs to them was Mr Cyril Thornber not wanting to run intensive stock, because they had always been used to free range. I told the representative that we wouldn't go back to free range, not now, because it was such a success keeping them intensively, and Mr Dove said at that point, "Well, I will go back and see what Mr Thornber has to say about it."

Eventually he came back, about two weeks later with the answer and he said that he was quite prepared to try just two buildings to be used to rear intensive breeding stock. So we tried it for one year and the results came back very satisfactory, so they were very happy to have the whole poultry site for their intensive breeding. We finished with a total of 25,000 breeding stock and I'm almost certain when I say that that was the beginning of intensive breeding for Thornber's; we started it. Our hatchability from the eggs kept from intensive breeding stock averaged anywhere between 84% - 91% hatchability, and so from these results, Thornber's started to run all their farms on intensive breeding methods. So it turned out to be a turning point both for us and for Thornber's, as they were then able to cover the whole of the country with their chicks in large numbers.

Thornber's were in the business of building poultry houses and from this new start and change of mind from free range to intensive breeding, they started to design new poultry houses known as 'controlled environment' for breeding stock. In 1963 we bought one of the first new houses for breeding from Thornber's. It was 84ft long and 38ft wide and it cost £1,800, delivered and erected. So from then we started to take all of our old ex-RAF buildings down to replace them with the new Thornber's controlled environment houses for poultry. In 1964, we bought another controlled environment house, which was 216ft long by 38ft wide and it was delivered and erected for £5000. This was quite a big building in those days and I remember its delivery very clearly because one of our men on the farm said to me, "If you can get over this expense, you can get over anything!" and I shall never forget that. So that was the start of a completely new era in poultry farming and as time went by, we kept putting more of these new houses up and taking the ex-RAF buildings down. The only two that I didn't like to see being taken down were the two buildings that the Dambusters crews were billeted in. We knew they had to come down and so they did, but to me it was such a shame. Little did we know back then how valuable they would have been to us with the Museum if we had kept them. Unfortunately, we had to take them down to make room for a more controlled environment. Looking back it really was a big shame to have got rid of them.

So time went by and we were growing and building. Naturally, my children were growing older and so was my father. He would spend all his time cleaning the hatching eggs and packing. Somewhere between 1960 and 1964, we changed houses; Father came to live in our pre-fab and Betty, Phillip, the twins and I went to live in the house on the big farm, so that I was closer to the poultry. We were being kept very busy with our poultry and in 1967, we decided to put up a completely new poultry farm, which was actually not far from the pre-fab that Betty and I first lived in when we were married. This was quite a major step forward for our business, because it was brand new from scratch. The poultry houses were 300ft long by 38ft wide and in 1970, we put up two battery cage houses for rearing pullets, which were to house the new type of bird, the 707 breeding stock and the 404 breeding stock from day old chicks to point-of-lay pullets, for commercial production. The total cost of this new site was £13,999.

I would just like to leave the poultry for the moment, to tell you a little story about Phillip that I am reminded of on the topic of new sheds. Before Phillip started school in 1963, aged 5, he had loved coming with me around the poultry and every year we would creosote the buildings, with a coloured wash which soaks into the wood walls and prevents rot. He always wanted to help me, even to creosote, so I gave him a little bucket and a small brush and he would help me to creosote these sheds; he seemed to love doing it! So when he started school, I had to fetch him home from school one particular day, in the car. When I arrived at school, Miss Ellis, the infant teacher, was walking Phillip by his hand to meet me in the car park. Miss Ellis said to me, "Mr Panton, Phillip made me smile today." I said, "Oh did he Miss? What happened?" "Well," she said "Today, we were going to have some painting lessons for the first time and I said to Phillip, "Can you paint Phillip?" and he said to me, "No, I can't paint Miss, but I can creosote!" So this is how precise he was, even at five years old, and that even made me smile.

Going back to the poultry again, my father-in-law retired when he turned seventy and he decided that he would like to go into supplying hatching eggs to Thornber's. So he sold all his arable farming equipment and left his one hundred acres of land, which had always been a council holding. He bought a bungalow with a twenty acre plot of land, which was only a mile down the road from us, so that he could keep his own chickens. So he left the house that Betty had grown up in and moved with Mrs Clement to this new land to keep chickens, closer to us. He had officially retired, but he just went into a different type of work to keep himself busy! He was a very hard working chap, Mr Clement. So we informed Thornber's, who were still wanting breeders to supply hatching eggs, as they were growing in strength, so they decided to take him on as a breeder, in a small way. When he became established with his breeding stock it, soon became quite interesting and, to some degree, quite annoying, because with our poultry we were doing everything to the text book; feed hoppers, water fountains, everything was done precisely, but Mr Clement was just the opposite. If you like, he was more like Heath Robinson, because he never had the proper amount of drink fountains, or feed hoppers, etc, that the building required for the number of birds. But when it came to hatchability, the results, which we would receive every week, he would always get a better hatchability rate than us. He was never below 87% and one week, I remember, he was 94%! But this was no flash in the pan, this was averaging! And I could never, ever fathom out how he could beat us. I came to the conclusion that the only reason could be his stockmanship. Our poultry were fed ad lib, (to be fed ad lib is a common poultry term used to describe when food is down for the birds all the time.) whereas Mr Clement would only feed and water his birds three times a day. His birds would always look very well and we never seemed to be able to compete with his hatchability rate. This used to be a very sore point because breeders were paid on the hatchability. His were reared intensively, the same as ours, in his ex-RAF buildings, so I thought that it must have been down to the number of birds. You see, he was able to do it all by hand, whereas we had to do it all automatically and this used to really aggravate us; we daren't do it like that because of the money involved, but he did, and he got the results! Bear in mind that by this stage, Mr Clement was eighty nine years old and he carried on until he was ninety seven years old! At the age of 92, he would even drive to Scotland and back on his own, so that he could see his daughter! And another thing I will tell you about this amazing man is that he never, ever wore glasses during the whole of his life. Sometimes he would come and help us work in the field with the sugar beet and it didn't matter how hot it used to get at times, he would never ever have a drink of water or tea in between meals like we would. He could just keep going; he was self-fuelling, if you like.

So back to 1969 and our new site. Altogether, the two poultry sites cost us £35,000 and it was so much more expensive than previously because of all the feeders and steel cages. At this stage, we had to put a manager in to look after it for us and the person we gave this job to was my good friend, Derek Hipkin, who I used to go running with. This was something completely new to Derek. He had just decided to call it a day with his grocers shop, so he had gone from a grocery and hardware shopkeeper to a poultry farm manager. He thought that he could manage to look after this poultry site, so we engaged Derek to come and look after it for us and he turned out to be one of the best; very conscientious at what he did and he made a first class poultry man. There were two buildings on site, as I have said; 150ft long by 32ft wide and they were smaller because they were battery houses. Everything was running smoothly with our new battery-house chicken sheds, Harold was well settled and we were working together very well indeed. We decided to consolidate, with the poultry for a few years with the supplying of hatching eggs to Thornber's.

Fred, Harold and Phillip

Chapter Thirteen

Brothers Reunited

Fred's mission to Germany.

I'm now going to take you forward to July 1971, when Father had completely retired at seventy five years of age, though he still liked to come down to help pack eggs in our egg packing room. Now, this particular year, we were having a very hot summer and I shall never, *ever* forget that night. I had to go and look at one of our poultry sites, at about 7 o'clock in the evening and I rode on my bicycle to check that the poultry were healthy and well. I went to see that the fans were all running and the birds weren't suffering with the heat and when I got up to the farm, my mother and father were sitting outside on chairs in the evening sun, because it was such a beautiful night. So when I was riding up to one of the sheds, just past the bungalow, Father stood up and waved me across to him and he obviously wanted to see me.

I called out to him and said, "I'll be there in five minutes, I just want to have a look at the chickens." Once I had finished looking round the birds, I went back to Father to see what he wanted and as soon as I got back to where Mother and Father were sitting in their chairs, Father said to me, "Now Fred, what I want you to do is this; I want you to go to Germany and get me a photograph of Chris's grave." I was so taken aback and pleased, I said straight away, "I *will* Dad. I've been wanting to do that for thirty years." I could not believe what he had just said to me, because he had never, ever wanted me to go. I was pleased to think that I would be going to find my brother's resting place and the prospect really excited me. I thought about all the things I had to do on the farm and worked out that the earliest I could possibly go was the 9th of September, just three months away! That was the plan, but at this stage we had no idea where Chris was buried, because Father had been upset to such a degree when we had first heard the news about Chris, that he didn't want to know anything more about any of it. I started thinking about all the arrangements which needed to be made and, suddenly it dawned on me that I'd never been abroad in my life and couldn't speak a word of German!

I decided that I would go and see my good friend, Derek Hipkin, who, as I've mentioned already, was now managing one of our poultry sites.

Derek said that he'd love to join me, so we planned it so that Harold would look after the site for a while and Derek could come with me as a mate. We were going to go in a little Renault 4L car and camp on convenient German camping sites.

Our plans were set for us to leave on the 9th September 1971. However, the big thing now was, we still had no idea where to find Chris or the place where he'd crashed. So we came to the conclusion that we would have to get all the information from the Ministry and the Records Office before we could go. That was bothering me just a bit, because I was wondering whether they would actually have all the information that I wanted. Anyway whilst I was trying to find out where I had to write to for all this information, I was reading one of our monthly poultry magazines, all about the poultry industry. I was just looking through the pages, when I saw, in big letters, the headline, "POULTRY FARMER TURNS AUTHOR". The story was about a man called Martin Middlebrooke of Boston, Lincolnshire, which happened to be only ten miles from Stickford, where we lived. And he was a poultry farmer, the same as me. It went onto say that Mr Middlebrooke had written a book on the battle of the Somme and was now writing a book on the Nuremberg Raid. I was so surprised that I read it again and I thought to myself, "That was the night that Chris went missing when he was shot down on the Nuremberg raid, March 31st 1944." While I was reading this book, I had a knock on my door and when I went to see who it was, it was a food representative selling poultry feed, which was vitamealo concentrates for poultry. While we were talking he said to me, "Do you know Martin Middlebrooke of Boston?" to which I replied "No, but it's a funny thing you should mention him, because I've just been reading how he was now turned author, in the poultry magazine". I told him that he was at the moment writing a book on the Nuremberg raid, and I said, "That's the night my brother was killed," and this rep said to me, "Really? Do you mind if I give him a call and tell him?" and, of course, I said, "No, I don't mind!" So this food rep gave Mr Middlebrooke a ring during the day and that night, Mr Middlebrooke rang me himself. He asked me if I was the brother of the Pilot Officer Christopher Whitton Panton, Flight Engineer, and, of course, I told him that I was. So he asked me if I minded if he came to see me the next morning. I didn't mind at all, as you can imagine. In fact, I was very pleased about this, so we arranged a time for him to call round and see me. When he arrived, we went into the house to talk and to my amazement, this man knew so much about my brother and his flying days

100

and where he had crashed and was first buried in 1944, to when he had been taken to Durnbach war cemetery, near Munich. I told him that I was planning to travel to Germany in September, but I had no idea where he had crashed, or anything about it, and he said to me, "I can give you all the information you want in order to go to Germany." He told me that Chris's plane had crashed on top of a very high range of hills near a little village called Friesen, about 9km from a town called Bamberg. Then, after telling me all this, he arranged to have all the information, maps and drawings for us to take to Germany, which saved me having to go to the ministry or do any of it myself and I thought to myself how really generous that was.

Eventually, the 9th September arrived and it was time to begin our journey to Germany. We were only going to stay for ten days, because we had to get back for our poultry, so we had all our camping gear on the roof rack and all our rations and clothes in the car. We started off at 10 o'clock in the morning, on the Friday, to go from Stickford to Harwich and from Harwich across the water to Ostend, in Belgium. When we approached Ostend it had just gone 9 o'clock at night and we were still quite a way out at sea. We could see all the coast of Ostend in the dark and how it was all lit up for miles with lights and I said to myself for the first time, "Have I got to drive through there?" because there was just a mass of high buildings and I was feeling very fearful, thinking "Shall we be able to understand the road signs for getting onto the autobahn, to get to Bamberg?" Derek had the map in front of him and when we came to the road signs, we could both just roughly guess what they meant... and luckily for us, we were right! We carried on driving all through the night, never stopping. We'd started at 10 o'clock on the Friday morning and we never stopped driving, until we got to about half past three in the morning and it had started to come in foggy and misty and we decided to stop somewhere that we could camp for the night. We found somewhere that looked like a big area of grass, so we pulled over onto this grass and put our tent up, next to a few little lights on the road and we had a rest until daylight broke the next morning.

The next morning we cooked ourselves a bit of breakfast with the little gas stove that we had brought with our camping equipment. On this grass patch that we had camped on, there were small trees and bushes and as day was breaking we were beginning to get traffic building up on the road, and everyone seemed to be blowing their hooters at us. Now, we had GB on the back of the car, which everybody would have been able to see and I asked Derek, who was just as baffled as I was, "Why is everyone blowing their horns at us?" and as daylight came through more and more, we could see that without realising we had parked on a roundabout! It was so big that you couldn't tell that it was a roundabout at night and in the fog… And of course you weren't supposed to park on it! When we realised what we had done, you can imagine that we couldn't get packed up quick enough, before we were arrested. We just couldn't believe that we had parked on a roundabout, but what with it being so misty and foggy you just couldn't tell!

So we then started making our way to our destination, our main camping site near the quite large town of Bamberg. We found the site that we were looking for in Bamberg and got ourselves booked in at about half past one in the afternoon, on the Saturday. I believe it was just over eight hundred miles from Stickford to Bamberg and we had just driven and driven. We got our tent all pitched up with the groundsheet and our two little beds and got ourselves nicely settled in. I knew that we were only 9km, less than 6 miles, from the crash site and, in the distance, I could even see the big range of hills, which is where the crash would have taken place. So, after we'd had a rest, after driving all those miles in such a short time, I said to Derek, "I don't think I can wait until tomorrow to find this crash site. It's only 6 miles away and I think we should go and have a look, ready for tomorrow." It was so exciting to me to believe that I was in Germany, so close to where my brother had crashed all those years ago. So we got in the car and headed towards the little village of Friesen. This was a very hilly part of Germany and as we approached the foothills, I could see that the slopes were really heavily wooded. So I said to Derek, as we were riding around the hills with all these old trees, "You would be able to see from here where a Halifax had crashed." I'd seen at East Kirkby where Lancasters had crashed, so I knew the size of area that a crash site would look like and, as we were driving and looking, we eventually saw a big space with no trees. So I said to my friend, "That looks like the size of a place that a Halifax could have crashed," We drove over to have a look at the gap in the trees, but before long we hit a problem and had to stop. The thing was, there was this very large grass field that we had to cross before we could get to the bottom of the foothills and, of course, this meant having to get permission in order to cross it and we couldn't see anyone to ask if it was all right. Eventually I said to Derek, "I think we'll have to take a risk and chance going across." So we opened this big gate and drove across the big grass field, hoping that no-one would come across and stop us. We got out of the car and looked across at the spot where we thought an aeroplane could have crashed. We found this hill to be nearly all limestone, which we could tell because of the colour of the white stone, and it was a very high and very jagged hill. So we took our bearings and glanced at where this crash could have been, and started walking up to get to it. We found the spot and we felt sure we were in the right area because Martin Middlebrooke had given us all the details before we left. We knew it was 9 kilometres from Bamberg, North-East on top of a hill, but when we arrived and looked at this site, I said to Derek, "I am sure that this is not a crash site at all, Derek." It certainly looked like one, but I was convinced that a plane had not crashed in the area where we were standing. So we made our way back down the hill to our vehicle and when we got in the car to drive away, I said, "You mark my words Derek, we shall find someone, before long, who can speak English."

We were just driving away to get back to the road, right in the middle of the field, when we saw two people at the very far end of it and I said to Derek, "We'll just drive across and ask if they can speak English, to see if we can get to know any information." When we got to them, it was a man and a woman who happened to be mushrooming, and at this point it would have been between five or six o'clock at night, and they would have been about fifty years of age. I turned my window down to speak to this German man, and I asked him, "Excuse me, can you speak English?" to which he said, "Just a little"; but I am sure that he could speak English better than I can! So I told him who I was and what I was doing here and what I was looking for, and then I gave him some particulars that Mr Middlebrooke had given to me. It turned out that we were simply in the wrong place. The village of Friesen was about three miles away, just around the bend of the foothills and we couldn't see it because it was just tucked away at the bottom of the foothills. It also transpired that this man was the brother-in-law of the Burgomaster of the village of Friesen, the very man that we had wanted! And he said to me, "I'll write you this little note and if you take it to the Burgomaster (who was the equivalent of a mayor) he'll give you all the information that you need." He told us where the Burgomaster lived and then, while he was writing this note for us, he suddenly stopped and said, "No, I won't, I'll take you myself." At this point, his wife came over to me and said, "My mother and father were killed during the war, when a Lancaster bomber crashed on top of my house and killed them both. What was that for?" I can tell you that this created quite an atmosphere for a few moments, because she looked at me right in the eye when she said it, and she *meant* it, because she said it twice, "What was that *for?*" You'll understand that it took quite a bit of answering such a direct question and, of course, I couldn't say that *their* air force had killed thousand in London and all of our cities, but we managed to sort it all out nicely, anyway.

So then, the brother-in-law took Derek and me to meet the Burgomaster and it turned out that he was a farmer himself, so we had something in common before we even started! Now, when the Burgomaster was told who I was, what I wanted and what I was looking for, in some respects he was pleasantly surprised. He told me that he used to be in the army himself and was in a prisoner of war camp near Ripon, North Yorkshire. He found this amazing because Chris was stationed at Skipton-on-Swale Airfield, which is no more than five to six miles from Ripon. He had been a prisoner so close to the airfield where Chris had been stationed. I'll just say that the night that Chris went to bomb Nuremberg and was shot down, Britain lost ninety four bombers; Lancasters and Halifaxes, as I had said before, and according to Mr Middlebrooke, my brother was the seventy sixth bomber to be shot down that night, on their 30th and final mission. The wreckage from this one Halifax, Chris' Halifax, covered all of 600 metres. All the pieces of the wreckage fell about the hill and some on the village. The fuselage, which was the biggest part, the front cabin section of the plane, fell on top of the hill, about to drop to the other side when it just stopped on top. The pieces covered the village and the plateau of the hilltop. It was a vast wreckage area.

After we had talked to the Burgomaster for some time, he kindly suggested that if Derek and I returned at 10 o'clock the following morning, he would take us to the top of the hill on his tractor and show us exactly where my brother's Halifax had crashed. He told us that there were two seats in the front of the tractor and he would put two more on the back for Derek and me, so there would be the Burgomaster himself, the publican who had seen the Halifax crash and Derek and me. So we arrived promptly at 10 o'clock on the Sunday morning and, sure enough, he was waiting to take us to the top of this big winding hill which must have been a mile and a half from the foothills to the top. When we got right to the top Derek and I were surprised to see that it was absolutely dead flat and all limestone. It was covered with moss and grass, small trees and bushes. We walked across to the crash site and he showed us where it all was and, because it was just mossed-over limestone, you could just use your foot to sweep aside the foliage to find pieces of the Halifax, still scattered on the ground. We actually got a plastic bag full of pieces left from my brother's aeroplane when we left. While we were up there and looking, I was thinking to myself, "He flew all the way from Skipton-on-Swale in North Yorkshire to crash on this range of hills in Germany; all that distance from Yorkshire to Friesen. I was reminded that Skipton-on-Swale, the airfield that he had been flying from, is also in the foothills of a very high range of hills, in the shadow of Sutton Bank. The hills in Friesen may be just that bit higher than the Yorkshire Hills, but it seemed that he went from one big lot of hills to another.

When we came back from the crash site to the little village, we got talking for a while to the two men who had accompanied us up the hill. The Burgomaster, as I have said, was a dairy farmer and the publican had a little public house in the village and it was the publican who told me that he had actually found the pilot, Chris Nielsen, who had escaped the crash. He had bailed out and this publican had found him in the churchyard, no idea where he was, crawling round on his hands and knees on a piece of grass which was about 40ft square.

The publican then showed me the exact spot where he had found Christian Nielsen, who looked to be in a terrible state, because he had landed through the branches of trees in the village on his way down and he looked to be cut a lot about the face. However, when they got him washed and cleaned, it wasn't as bad as it had looked; it was just grazes and scratches. The wireless operator, Harry Cooper, landed right on top of the hill where the plane had crashed, but on his way down he had lost one of his flying boots and there was eighteen inches of snow on top of the hill that night. Jack McLauchlan, who was the rear gunner, bailed out and landed in a grass field in the valley, just outside the village of Friesen. All three men were captured and taken to the little dance hall in the village, under guard until the police arrived from Bamberg. They were then taken to the police station for one week to be interrogated.

After we had spent quite some time speaking to the Burgomaster and the publican, they told us that the rest of the crew, the other five members, who were killed, were taken by hearse and buried under some fir trees in a corner of the local cemetery. This cemetery was about a mile and a half away, in a very small village called Butenheim. I was very surprised and pleased when the publican gave me a photograph, taken in 1944, of the two horses, the hearse and the two men who had taken the bodies to the cemetery. After the war, in 1948, the bodies were removed from Butenheim and reinterred at Durnbach war cemetery, near Munich.

Derek and I said goodbye and thanked the Burgomaster and his friend, the publican, then made our way to Butenheim cemetery, to see where the bodies were first buried. We soon found the place and I must say that it was the most beautifully, well-kept cemetery that I have ever seen. You really have to admire the Germans for how they look after their local cemeteries with such care and respect. We looked around for a while, then decided to make our way back to the campsite at Bamberg to make ourselves a meal and get well rested, because the next morning we had a journey of 200 miles to find Durnbach War cemetery... to find the final resting place of Chris and the rest of the crew. We made our meal and got rested up as much as we could, to be ready for an early start on Monday morning. We knew the journey would take us several hours, so, next day we packed up our tent and all of our belongings as quickly as we could and got on our way to a campsite on the outskirts of Munich, knowing that Durnbach war cemetery is only thirty miles away.

We found the camping site, where we stayed for two nights, and we seemed to be in a lonely spot in the area, but we had picked it because it was quiet and dimly lit at night. The following morning when we woke up, we got ourselves some breakfast and, because I was getting very anxious and couldn't wait to find Durnbach, we were on our way by 9 o'clock. The cemetery is said to be in one of the prettiest places in Germany and I would wholeheartedly agree. When we arrived it certainly seemed that way to us. It was all nicely settled in this lovely area with the Austrian mountains in the distance and it just could not have been in a nicer setting. When we arrived in the parking area of the cemetery we could see all of the gravestones; just over three thousand airmen were buried in this place and as we walked in, we could see how beautiful, clean and tidily it was all kept. We had the directions of where Chris was buried; the row letters and grave numbers and I just couldn't wait to find my brother's grave. Then, after about ten minutes of methodical searching, we found row G and all we had to do was work our way down, looking at the names, until we eventually found my brother and the crew. All five members are together with their own stones. When I found my brother's grave it said 'Pilot officer Christopher Whitton Panton, Flight Engineer' and his number and date of death of 31st March 1944. When I got to it I went to put my hand on his gravestone and I knelt down and it's difficult for me to really tell you how I felt. I knew that I was within six feet of my brother, and I want to tell you now, that while I was looking at his grave, all of the memories of the war years and all my memories of my brother came flooding back to me. It renewed all of my previous interests in the Second World War. You see, to be within six feet of my brother again, after all these years, was really quite something to me. Then I looked at the graves of the rest of the crew, the navigator, the mid-upper gunner, the bomb aimer, Chris the flight engineer and the second pilot. When I came to leave the cemetery, I walked backwards to the car park and I never took my eyes off the graves, because I thought that I might never see them again in my life. When we got into the car again to drive away, I still could not take my eyes off the cemetery until it went out of my sight. We headed back to our camping site near Munich and, even though we were feeling very tired by that point, we had to get a meal ready and get rested up, because the next morning we would be getting up early again and moving on for another long drive. We would be going through parts of Austria, and Switzerland on the way home. I'll just say that by this stage, from the time we left the boat at Ostend to drive through to Bamberg, I had driven five hundred miles before I became really confident of driving in Germany, but by now I had complete confidence in driving on the right hand side of the road!

I'll just tell you, we had quite a frightening experience that night. We'd just had our meal and settled down for the night to have a sleep. It was very dark and our camping site, as I said, was very dimly lit. I was lying on a camp bed and Derek was on a ground sheet to the side of me. Derek was soon fast asleep and snoring quite a bit, whereas I was finding it hard to sleep, thinking about everything we had done during the day. Our tent wasn't too far from one of the lights on the campsite and at about 2 o'clock in the morning, I saw somebody walking round the tent, trying to find his way into the entrance of our tent, and that made me very anxious. Our tent had a zip-fastening at the front and I was thinking to myself, "I hope he doesn't find the zip." I could see this big shadow walking round us two or three times, and at that point, I shouted out loud, "Derek, *Derek!* There's somebody trying to get in." But I couldn't get him to wake up; he just carried on snoring away. Eventually, this person found the zip to the tent and he opened it right up and as soon as he had opened it, he dived straight in, landing between Derek and me. Of course I was nearly petrified, but I remembered that I had a good, big torch right to the side of me. This man didn't say a thing, he just lay between us, so I got my torch and I shone the light on him and I said, "What do you think you're doing? You shouldn't be in here," but he reckoned that it was his tent, and not ours! So naturally I wanted to get him out the tent as quickly as I could, so I said to him, "Look, you take my torch and go and look for your tent." I gave him the torch and when he took it, he shone the light right onto Derek's face and eyes. Derek must have been half-conscious because he said, "*Will* you put that light out?" but this man just stood there shining this light on poor Derek's face. I eventually got him out and he took my torch, looking for another tent and, sure enough, he found another one; a smaller one, only half the size of ours. He went to it and there only seemed to be a little flap over the front and this man just dived straight in it, the same as he had into ours! I thought to myself, "There's going to be some eruptions there in a moment!" So, I stood there watching, but there wasn't a sound, though it was a very low tent. Derek woke up soon after and I told him everything that had happened and I was so annoyed because I ended up not getting a wink of sleep that night, watching the tent across from us. This man had my torch you see, and it started to bother me because I didn't want to get blamed for something I hadn't done. So I watched this tent all night to make sure he never came out, because I wanted my torch back.

At half past three in the morning, a security guard came walking across the campsite, so I called him over and told him what had happened and pointed to the tent where the intruder now was. I asked the officer whether he would mind going to retrieve my torch from this person, but he said he could not because he wasn't allowed to do things like that. So all I could do was sleep with one eye open and rest as much as I could until daylight the next morning. When morning came, we had our breakfasts and started to do our washing and packing, all the while I was keeping an eye on this tent. It was now daylight and we'd never seen anybody or heard a sound, but just before we'd finished packing up, with our tent on the roof rack of the vehicle, I looked across and saw that this tent was one that you blow up with a foot pump and it had started deflating, gradually going down and down and down and I said to Derek, "I don't think there's anyone in that tent." It continued going down further until it got to about eighteen inches from the ground, when we started to see some movement. We could see somebody's elbow raising and fumbling about and we could see that there were two people in this small, deflated tent and they eventually came struggling out, so that we could see it was the man that I had given my torch to. I went across to him, and thought to myself that I'd better be nice to him. I said,

"Have you finished with that torch of mine? I let you borrow it to look for your tent, but could I have it back now please?" He gave it back, and what it was, we hadn't known at the time, but it was the Munich beer festival! The place was full of beer stands and celebrations and we hadn't known, so there was this big mix up!

I wasn't very happy though, because we still had a long drive in front of us and I hadn't had any sleep yet. We drove through Austria, and Switzerland, onto another camping site, where we stayed for two nights, so that we could go sightseeing. On the second night, around 9 o'clock at night, I said to Derek, "I think we ought to check how many miles it is from here to Ostend." You see we were thinking of staying another night, but I thought that we ought to check, as we had to be at the dock at 9 o'clock in the morning and I didn't want to miss the ferry. So we got the map out and put it on the bonnet. Derek was navigating and he came to the conclusion that it would be roughly four hundred miles, which we decided would be all right, but I just said again that I thought we should double check and it's a good job that we did, because it turned out to be just over seven hundred miles! So I said that we couldn't leave it until tomorrow night, we would have to start back tonight. We packed everything up as quickly as possible and had to drive all through the night until we got back into France.

During the night there came a very thick fog, which made it hard work driving, but the one good thing was that there wasn't much traffic on the road, which meant that I was able to drive down the centre of the road, on the yellow markings as much as I could. There were steep slopes and drops on these hills, so driving down the middle was the safest thing. We had to have a stop for a rest, so we pulled over in a big parking area at the side of the road, and we stayed until daylight. I needed a break because I was starting to turn too dizzy and tired for driving, so we decided to get some rest. Derek climbed into the back of the vehicle to lie down and I had all the front seats, with my head on the window, trying to rest. It was very dark and there was a very thick fog and Derek soon fell asleep again and was busy snoring away, when we had another little 'experience.' Suddenly I heard the sound of what sounded like somebody letting the wind out of our tyres; I heard a pssssssshhhhhhh noise and I was absolutely certain that somebody was letting our tyres down. At first, I spoke very quietly, "Derek, *Derek!* Someone's letting the wind out of our tyres." Derek continued to snore and I heard the sound again of more air releasing, and I thought "There goes another" and there even seemed to be a creak in the car. I had my head against the window and I was sure someone was about to break the glass in. I expected someone to hit me on the back of the head, but I didn't have the strength to pull myself away from the window. I was so frightened that all my strength seemed to have left my body, so I couldn't move, even though I wanted to! The whole car seemed to lurch with this noise, I was so certain of what was happening. I continued hearing this noise, just like the wind being let out of the car tyres and it came again for a third time. Eventually, after a while, we got ourselves gathered together, as it started to become lighter with the breaking morning. I pulled myself together and opened the door to get out the vehicle. Both Derek and I got out and to my surprise, all of our tyres were all right, no one had tried to let the air out, they were still good. But while we were still outside, we found out what the noise was. A little further down the road, there was another parking area for cars and lorries and it was the air brakes from these lorries, which, from the inside of our car and with the thick fog cushioning the sound, really did sound like someone letting the air out of our tyres.

So we started on the road again to Ostend, as we now just had to finish driving through Belgium, which meant that we had an easy day's driving that day. We had planned to stay one night in Ostend on a camp site, ready for the ferry journey at 9 o'clock the next morning. By 11 o'clock in the morning all the fog from the night before had cleared and it was a lovely sunny day to drive through the countryside. There were hills on both sides of the road, so we decided that we would stop for a walk. We pulled the car over at the side of a hill, took some food and drink and stopped for around half an hour or so. While we were sitting there, nearly every car that drove past us blew their horns at us, again! We couldn't understand at the time why they were doing this and so, eventually, we got up and made our way back to the car to head to the campsite at Ostend. Later, whilst in Ostend, we found out that we should not have been in this field, sitting and having a picnic because it was dangerous, as we were at risk of catching rabies. If an infected animal that had the disease had left any of their saliva on the grass and we had put our hands in it, we were very likely to catch rabies, which of course we hadn't thought of, or even known about.

So the next morning, the ferry came for 9 o'clock, as scheduled, and we arrived back at Harwich on Saturday. We'd been exactly ten days, as planned, from start to finish, getting home for about 8 o'clock at night. Mission accomplished! I came back, somehow with a new spirit in me.

Postcard from Bamberg

Halifax crash site   Chris's original burial place in Butenheim

Chris's final resting place with his comrades at Durnbach War Cemetery

Chapter Fourteen

My Mission to Find the Lost Crew

We checked the mileage on the car and from start to finish, we had done over 2200 miles! This gives you some idea of the distance that we had been driving every day. So once I had been home and had seen my wife and children, I went to visit my mother and father to let them know that we were back and we had plenty of photographs in the camera to be developed during the week. Now, on the following Monday morning, I went up to one of the farm sites to check our poultry and this Monday, I shall never forget because it started the beginning of a long journey in my life. I went into the egg packing room and we had a lady who worked for us, Madge Bailey. When I got into the packing room the first thing she said to me was, "Good morning Fred, how did you get on in Germany?" and I said, "I got on very well thank you Madge. Everything went according to plan." To which she replied, "Good. Fred, I've got something for you to look at that I think you might be interested in." She walked over to her coat, which was hanging on a peg on the other side of the room. She put her hand in one of the pockets and pulled out a Sunday newspaper cutting and handed it to me. I opened it out and looked at it and there was a picture of a Lancaster and the caption read in big letters, "LANCASTER BOMBER FOR SALE. SQUIRES GATE, BLACKPOOL." I read it and I said to her, "Madge, You couldn't have given me this at a better time. I'm going to see if I can buy that."

"Just Jane" for sale at Squires Gate, Blackpool

113

You see, all my interests in the War had been rekindled since my trip to Germany. My father had not been interested in 1949 in a Halifax Bomber, but now this Lancaster was up for sale, I was determined to buy it! So after only ten days of being home, I made plans to go to Squires Gate, Blackpool to have a look at this Lancaster. Madge's husband, Bill, took me to view it. I was very surprised at the good condition that it was in and found out that it was to be sold at auction about three weeks later. So, I went back to Squires Gate, Blackpool for a second time for the auction and I went to the sale with all arms ready! However, the auction had just started, the lot number of the Lancaster had been called and they were just about to start the bidding, when, all of the sudden, the auctioneer announced, "Sorry Gentlemen, we will have to withdraw this item from the auction," and the Lancaster was withdrawn before I'd even had a chance to bid for it! As many as 100 people had come to the auction, interested in purchasing the Lancaster and all of them were very surprised and disappointed that it had been withdrawn, especially me! During the three weeks between my having been to view the Lancaster and the actual auction, the Right Honourable Lord Lilford had bought it privately. Of course, I was very disappointed at this withdrawal because I had wanted to buy it so much. So after finding all this out I contacted Lord Lilford and had to speak through his agent, who was a man called Mr Bracewell, living near Preston, Lancashire. I got on very nicely with him and he told me that if ever they did decide to sell the Lancaster, then they would give me the first refusal. I had to wait another twelve years until 1983 before this opportunity came about and in those twelve years, it had been moved to RAF Scampton as a gate guardian; Lord Lilford had loaned it to the Air Force in 1973. So in 1983 he told me that he was prepared to sell it and I, of course, bought it, although in those twelve years, as you can imagine, the price had altered quite a lot!

When I had first returned from Germany, I'd been to see my mother and father to tell them we had had a successful trip and managed to take the photographs that Father had wanted. It took a little time to get them all developed, but when I did take them to show my mother and father, we decided that we would pick four photographs out of the lot, to be framed. We chose one of the crash-site on top of the hill, one where Chris was first buried at Butenheim Cemetery, one of the Burgomaster, the Publican and myself and then the photograph of the grave where he was reburied at Durnbach war cemetery near Munich in 1948. We had them enlarged and put them in one frame for Father, which took a few weeks to be done, but then I took him these four photographs and put them on the wall, directly opposite where he used to sit in his chair near the fire, so that he could see them all the time. Only three weeks from that day of taking them and putting them on the wall, Father died in his sleep and that came as a very great shock to me. It also convinced me that he knew something that I didn't know; to have me go and fetch him those photographs. That's one thing I shall never forget because I am sure that he knew, knowing my Father as well as I did. I really thought a lot of him, and I shall never, ever be the man that he was, because he gave me such a lot of good, sound advice. You see, I worked with him for forty years, and he only had to give me a look; every expression on his face told me whether I'd done right or wrong, he had no need to speak. We used to think, when Chris was doing his tour of operations, that if anything happened to him, then it would just about kill my mother, but when it did happen, it was the opposite way on. Mother took it like a soldier, but Father never really got over it and he took it the hardest because when Chris used to come home on leave and we'd all gone to bed, Father and Chris would sit up late while Chris told Dad about some of the operations he'd been on.

I would also like to share this with you; as you know, after coming back from Germany, all my interests had been renewed and the next thing I wanted to do was to try to meet up with the three crew who survived the crash: two Canadians and one Dane. Jack McClauchan, the Rear Gunner and Harry Cooper, the Wireless Operator, were both Canadian and Christian Nielsen, the Pilot, was Danish, but lived in America. These were the three members of my brother's crew who survived the crash on that fateful night of 31st March 1944, when we lost ninety four Lancaster and Halifax bombers in one operation. So I started to make plans to go to Canada to try and find them, but I had no idea which part of Canada, or where they lived.

However, luck came one day when Martin Middlebrooke, the author who had written the book on the Nuremberg raid, gave me a call on the telephone and told me that he had just received a letter from Mr Harry Cooper, the Wireless Operator, to tell him that he had been involved in the Nuremberg raid. You see, Martin Middlebrooke had advertised in the press, in Canada, as to whether anybody had been flying that night; March 31st 1944, and Cooper answered that yes, he had. But Martin told me that when he wrote back to Cooper for any information on that night they had flown to Nuremberg, he never answered the letter; he declined to give any information about the raid. That's the reason that he had rung me, to give me this information and to pass on Cooper's address for me to write to him. I did write to him, and he never answered my letter either. I told him who I was and that I was planning to come to Canada in 1974, a year before I was going to go, because I was just so interested to meet the Canadians who flew with my brother.

So now, how was I going to plan it? I just couldn't work it out! But I haven't mentioned that I did have a Canadian farmer friend, who I had known for three years and he came to see me once a year. His name was Mr Wendell Burns and he lived in Saskatchewan, in a small village called Wynyard, where he, his wife and his son-in-law farmed 5000 acres. He'd been in 408 squadron, Royal Air Force himself, as a bomb aimer, flying Halifaxes and Lancasters from Linton-on-Ouse in Yorkshire. He told me that if I would like to go and see him in Saskatchewan and stay with him for a few days, he would take me to find my brother's wireless operator, Harry Cooper, at the address that I had in Vancouver, which was 1,300 miles from Wynyard. Wendell had a friend living there who was a retired school teacher, who also used to train navigators during the war. So that decided everything; the plan was to go and see Wendell Burns.

So, as I was saying, Mr Cooper never answered my letter and I thought, "Well, if he'd been living at this place since he was demobbed, I'm pretty sure he'd still be living there in 1974," so I decided to go to Canada in the May of 1974. I flew from Heathrow to Toronto and then by train on The Canadian National Railway right through to Wynyard. I believe that it was nearly a week in travelling; 5000 miles in round figures and I was met by Wendell in Wynyard. The flight and the journey by train through Canada was the experience of my life and then to go and live on Wendell's farm, which I enjoyed very much. However, before we could travel to Vancouver, he had to just finish his seed drilling, because it was spring time and he had to finish his crop. So he asked me to help him finish before we journeyed to Vancouver, to which I of course agreed, and loved doing. I like Canada very much and I used to think that I could go and live there at one time. Had I been a younger man, I would have been a farmer in Saskatchewan.

Eventually, the day came when we were going to set off for Vancouver by train, through the Rockies, Jasper, Kamloops, so you can imagine that it was quite exhilarating to think that we would soon be arriving in Vancouver to meet Wendell's friend and begin my little mission! Eventually, we arrived and were met by Wendell's good friend who picked us up by car and took us back to his house, where we stayed for two nights. I knew then that we were within only a few miles of Harry Cooper, wireless operator, which was very exciting. When we arrived back at the house I mentioned to Wendell's friend about trying to find Cooper's telephone number. We found the number at 1200 Mountain Highway and I told this friend of Wendell's that I had written to Harry Cooper one year earlier, but that he had never answered me and that he had never answered Martin Middlebrooke's letter either. So we decided that we had to be a bit careful as to how we would handle it and what we would say. So I asked him if he would ring and suggested to him, "Just say who you are, where you live and that you have a friend just passing through Vancouver called Fred Panton and would it be all right if we called in to see him." So he rang for me and Mr Cooper answered the phone. Wendell's friend told Cooper who he was and what he wanted, that I was just passing through and that I would very much like to see him, to which Cooper replied; "Yes, I'll see him, for five minutes." I thought "Yes, well that'll be all right. I've waited one year, I've travelled 6000miles to see him. That's quite all right for me!" We got in the car, the three of us, Wendell, his friend and I and we went to find 1200 Mountain Highway.

When we found it, Mr Cooper was outside watering his lawn. He had worked in the skiing industry ever since he was demobbed in 1945. When I left home, I had brought a book from Mr Middlebrooke, about the Nuremberg raid, all signed ready, especially for Mr Cooper. When we did make his acquaintance, we got on very well and we were asked into his house to meet his wife and to talk. When he saw me and got to know what I wanted, what I was after and he could see that everything was genuine, he wanted me to stop the night with them. After talking to Cooper about flying from Skipton-on-Swale and talking about the rest of the crew, it soon began to dawn on me that these Canadians were very genuine and very straight talking men and it was no wonder Chris enjoyed flying with the Canadians. Mr Cooper told me quite a few interesting stories about the days when they were flying and about that particular night, but he wouldn't enlarge too much. But after everything, I enjoyed talking to him very much, thinking to myself, "This person was the last man to see my brother alive and they had flown on all those operations together." He spoke very well of all the crew, especially the pilot. So after going to see him on this particular day, we then met again the next day and he took us out at night to have a meal. But the time came when we had to depart and go back to Wynyard, but before I left, I asked Mr Cooper the $64,000 question, "Can you tell me where Christian

Nielsen is living, because my brother thought a lot of his pilot and it would mean a lot to me to meet him." They had, after all, worked together and I was keen to catch up with Nielsen, very keen. Cooper told me that Nielsen was married with two daughters and was living at a place called La Grange near Chicago but that was all he knew. Nielsen used to send a Christmas card every year, but that had stopped some time ago. I also asked him if he could tell me where Jack McClauchlan was living, because Jack and Chris were friends in a big way. In fact, Jack wrote to my mother and father once he had come out of the prisoner of war camp, but we never, ever heard another word from him afterwards. Cooper replied that the last time he had heard from McClauchlan was twenty years ago and that he was living in Winnipeg at that time. I thought, "When we get back to Wynyard, I shall have to drive back through Winnipeg to get back to Toronto to get home, I could stop one night in Winnipeg to look his number up in the telephone book to find him." So after leaving Wendell's friend's home and returning to Wynyard, I stayed a few more days with Wendell and then I had to make my way back to Toronto to fly back home. But I had made my mind up that I was going to stay in Winnipeg, which was four hundred miles from Wynyard, so that I just might find Jack McClauchlan.

Arriving at my new destination, I booked myself into the Canadian National Hotel and once I had checked myself into my room, I just lay on the bed for a few minutes. Then I got the phone directory and proceeded to look for a McClauchlan. Now, when Mr Middlebrooke was writing his book, he had told me that it was McLaughlin. Before that I had always understood that he was called McClauchlan, but he corrected me and was adamant that he was called McLaughlin. So I started to look through the names and when I rang the very first one, I told the operator who I was and that I was looking for a McLaughlin who had flown for the Royal Air Force during the Second World War, but I didn't know what his telephone number was. She was a very helpful person and she tried the first name, and proceeded to call all the McLaughins in Winnipeg, but there weren't any who had flown with the Royal Air Force. But she was so good that only charged me for the one telephone call, not all the names that she had rung which were to no avail.

So, I lay on the bed, disappointed, thinking that that was it. Then, all of a sudden, it struck me that Martin Middlebrooke could have been wrong and it could have been McClauchlan in the first place. I jumped up and got the telephone book again. I found it on the third name down; J. G. McClauchlan and I thought, "I bet that's him."

I rang the number and the telephone kept ringing and ringing and ringing before there was any answer and then it was a lady who had picked up the phone. I said, "Mrs McClauchlan?" She answered "Yes?" "Was your husband flying with the Royal Air Force during the Second World War?" and she told me, "Yes, he was. He was a Tail Gunner."

When I told her who I was, the brother to her husband's Flight Engineer, Chris Panton, she answered, "Really? Do you know, Fred, my husband has never stopped talking about your brother. He would *love* to meet you." I told her that I was very interested in meeting him as well. Unfortunately, her husband wouldn't be home until midnight, because he worked for the Yellow Pages directory and there was a strike on in Winnipeg with the telephone operators, so he'd volunteered to work the telephones. I told her that I'd just booked in at the Canadian National hotel in Winnipeg and she instantly replied, "Would it be possible to book yourself out and come and stop the night with us, so that Jack can see you?" I was very pleased and told her that it would be possible, so she said, "I'll come and pick you up in the car and bring you back home. But I'm not going to let Jack know that you're here; we won't say anything until we pick him up at midnight from the telephone exchange."

So the time came when we had to pick him up at midnight. The building he was working in was huge and we stopped on the opposite side of the road, in a very, very wide street; it would have been at least 60ft wide. We were sitting in the car waiting, when he eventually came out the door and started walking over to the car. Mrs McClauchlan and I got out to meet him and the first words she said to her husband were, "Now Jack, do you know who this fellow is?" He looked me up and down for a moment and eventually he said, "You wouldn't be a Panton would you?" Now, he'd never seen me in his life, but he got it in one! He said that it was my eyes that gave me away. "It's the same twinkle in your eyes that Chris had."

So we went home and had a bit of supper, while his wife went to bed and we stayed up talking until half past two in the morning. He told me countless stories about Chris, the crew and himself; which were so interesting. I'd like to share one little story that he told me about Chris and himself. He said he has never forgotten, "During our flying days, when we were going on operations, we had a little Austin car between us. Now, there used to be a little restaurant on the way to Harrogate, at Skipton-on-Swale and we used to go to this little restaurant for 'Two eggs and bacon for two shillings' which would have been quite a luxury in those days; it was a treat for any Aircrew that called in. So, we went this particular night that we weren't on operations and we ordered our meal of eggs and bacon and the restaurant owner brought our plates to the table. Chris then proceeded to pick up the salt and put it on his eggs, but the restaurant owner saw him do this and he said to Chris, "You shouldn't do that, it's the height of bad manners to pepper or salt your food before you taste it." Chris jumped up from the table and said to him, "It's the height of bad manners to criticize another at the table." With that, Chris walked out of the restaurant and just left his meal. I had to go out and persuade him to come back! When I left the forces after the war, got married and had my three daughters, I used to say to them while they were eating at the table, "Never, ever criticize another at the table, it's the height of bad manners." I'd never forgotten what Chrissy had said.

Another story he told me, was about when they bought the little Austin car. I don't know how much it cost, but I know that it wasn't a lot and I remember Father sending Chris a little money to help him buy it. The first time Jack and Chris went out in it, they found a little packet in the side pocket of the car. It said on it 'Gas Savers. Put one in at every fill.' They thought it was a bit odd, because the tablets in the packet smelled a lot like mothballs. But they thought, "Well, that's what it says, Put one in at every fill, save fuel." so they decided that they would try it and they put one in the petrol tank. One night shortly after, they were going to the restaurant on the way to Harrogate again, when the engine started stuttering and they had to pull the choke out a bit to keep it going. They had to keep pulling out the choke until eventually it stopped and they had to take the carburettor off to see what the problem was and why it didn't seem to be getting its petrol. They had a look and found that what they had put in were indeed mothballs! They also found the engine full of naphthalene flakes. The tablets weren't gas savers at all; someone had uncharitably written it on the packet! I used to tease Chris about it and say, "What type of a Flight Engineer are you supposed to be? Putting mothballs in an engine?"

Before I left McClauchlan, I said to him, "Now Jack, can *you* answer the $64,000 question? Can you tell me where Chris Nielsen is living now?" But he said exactly the same as Cooper had, that he hadn't heard from him for over two years and, even though he had easy access to all the telephone directories through his work and had tried to ring him lots of times, he had never been able to trace Pilot Nielsen again. Apparently he had moved on and he had never left any forwarding address, so, for the time being, that was the end of the line. Jack also told me that his pilot didn't want to know anything more about the war and that he had never really got over losing his crew. McClauchlan did think a lot of his pilot, but he had stopped wanting to know anything about the war; he had tried writing for a few years, and then sent Christmas cards only. But I should have loved to have known him because I know that my brother thought so much of him and I've heard that he was a very colourful character.

I think that I ought to say, that Wendell Burns was shot down over Hamburg himself. He was the Bomb Aimer and he and the Mid-Upper Gunner were the only two to get out and survive the crash. He bailed out and his parachute opened at exactly the same time as the Lancaster hit the ground. If it hadn't been for the wind blowing him sideways, he doesn't think that he would have made it. He broke his ankle when he landed, very near to a German Luftwaffe fighter airfield and the Germans picked him up and took him to one of their hospitals. The reason I'm telling you this story is that when he was in his hospital bed, he was next to the window, so he was able to gaze up at the sky. He had great admiration for the American pilots, because they went on their bombing missions during the daytime and on one particular day, when the sun was shining and the sky was clear, he could see three flying fortresses coming over, very, very high and leaving vapour trails behind them. They just shone like bits of silver, high up in the sky and, as he lay there in his bed, he watched all three being shot down. He saw the Germans do it; all three of those flying fortresses were shot down despite their great height in the sky. That's just one of the stories that he shared with me.

On another occasion, they had gone to bomb Berlin one night and he had just gone right down into the nose of the Lancaster ready to prepare for the bomb run, when he just happened to glance upwards only to see another Lancaster above them, with its bomb doors open, ready to drop a huge bomb! He had to warn his pilot to do a quick left turn or the bomb would have dropped right on top of them! He assured me that that never, ever happened to them again!

His Lancaster was a Mk2 Lancaster with radial engines. Only 301 of these Mk2 Lancasters fitted with radial engines were ever built, but Wendell told me that they could fly up to 1000ft higher than a Lancaster with the usual Merlin engine. It was only by chance that this was discovered. There happened to be a large surplus of these radials, which were built for Halifaxes, so they tried putting them on a few Lancasters as an experiment and found that they could go 1000ft higher. I learned a lot from meeting Chris's crewmates, but eventually, it was time to return home.

After arriving back from Canada and looking back on my time spent there, it had proved to be a great success. My interests were growing more and more with my excitement at the thought of being able to find my brother's remaining crew. It was making me more determined to find Christian Nielsen, Chris's pilot. It just seemed to me that he was now the final piece of the jigsaw puzzle for me to put together. But I had a feeling that I was going to have quite a job on my hands, because I didn't know where to start.

So I began by writing letters to all his previous addresses; I went through the records office, the Salvation Army, I went through everywhere to try and find him. You see, I was committed now and, although it was a testing time, I thought, "I've started now, so I have to finish it!" Fortunately, I was just so keen and interested to find Nielsen that it gave me all the energy I needed to keep going. I knew how much my brother thought of his pilot; he would talk about him a lot when he came home on leave and, of course, Nielsen himself came to visit my father after the war. He sent us Christmas cards for two years after that, but then we never had any contact again. So, to cut a long story short, I went through all the different available sources of contact, but all to no avail. I was searching and contacting, using different methods for a total of twelve years, from 1974 to 1986. Eventually, I did manage to get details of what was supposed to be Nielsen's latest address in Illinois, but the letter that I sent came back, 'returned to sender' saying that he was deceased. It appears that he had died six months previous to my letter; he had had a heart attack whilst playing squash, so I was told. I learned at a later date that he had, indeed, lost all interest in the war and I understand he never really got over losing his crew. As you can understand, it came as a hard blow to me to learn that after searching for him for twelve years, I had missed him by just six months. I realised that I had encountered two disappointments; losing the purchase of the Lancaster and missing Chris Nielsen by such a short time. I thought about it for a while and came to the conclusion that I might have to call it a day and so life carried on with our farming and our poultry, which we were progressively expanding every year. My brother Harold and I were both kept very busy every year with our business.

It was unfortunately around this time that we lost Betty's mother, Mrs Clement. She died in 1973, one year to the day exactly after my father had passed away, if you can believe it. This was obviously a very sad time for the family for we were all very close and we lived very near to one another. After she passed, Mr Clement would come to us for tea every night and after a few weeks of this Betty and I said that it would be much better if he came to live with us, rather than living on his own, on his big farm. So we had an extension built onto our house at Stickford and he moved in with Betty, me and our three children. He lived with us for eleven or twelve years and lived to be ninety seven years of age.

Fred's dad, Madge and Mr Clement

Mr Clement at Stickford

Fred's Visit to Canada

Harry Cooper

Bill Pooley, Harry Cooper and Fred

Harry Cooper and his wife Vivienne in Vancouver

Chapter Fifteen

The Biggest Adventure of my Life Begins

Now, Nielsen had died in 1986, but I would like to just take you back a step to 1981, to what would be the beginning of the biggest adventure of my life. I had a telephone call from a friend of mine who called to ask me, "Do you know that part of East Kirkby Airfield is up for sale privately?" It was the part which happened to have two poultry houses and the old, original control tower, which stood on the ex-RAF base. He said, "I hope you don't mind me ringing Fred, but I thought that you might be interested in buying it." This friend of mine was a man called Den Brown and his notifying me of the sale of East Kirkby Airfield, made him the first link in this great venture that I was about to begin. I thanked him very much for informing me and asked him if it was possible for me to go and have a look at the control tower and poultry houses. He assured me that it would be and so he made the arrangements for Harold and me to go and view this particular part of the airfield where the Lancasters used to fly from. So we looked around the poultry huts and then we were taken to view the old control tower, which I thought was still in fair condition for its age. We went inside to have a look at the different rooms and then went to stand on the balcony outside. I stood leaning on the railings looking round and I never said aloud to my brother or Den Brown, but I was thinking to myself that the only thing I was really interested in was the control tower. As I was standing there, looking round, I was imagining to myself that if I could buy this land, then this would be the real home for the Lancaster bomber, whenever Lord Lilford was prepared to sell. About one hundred and twenty metres from the control tower there used to be a big T2 Hangar, which would have held three Lancasters during the war. It had already been taken down, but to me it was all still intact and I thought to myself, "If I can buy this part of the airfield with the control tower and then get the Lancaster, bring her here and put another hangar up for her to live in, then there'll be nothing like it in the world." As far as I'm concerned if you want to look at a Lancaster bomber, the place to go and see one is where they flew from, not in a modern building in a city; the place to see it is where they were designed to fly from, an airfield. It's the only way you can truly get the atmosphere of what a bomber airfield would look like during the Second World War. That atmosphere would take you right back to 1944 - 1945. That was going to be my goal; to try and buy this part of the airfield. So Den gave me the information that I needed and I contacted the land agents who had been given the job of selling the piece of the airfield which I wanted. They told me that there was a second part of the airfield up for sale, at the opposite end to the control tower and chicken huts and they weren't prepared to sell one part without the other. They warned me that if we were really interested, then we had to buy all or nothing. That came as quite a surprise to me, because we were only interested in the site containing the control tower. But there was no way that they would sell one site without the other; so now I had to go away and make my mind up one way or the other whether I wanted both parts of the airfield. After a time, I decided that I would negotiate for both sites, with having poultry houses of our own already. So after discussing the value and prices, we eventually came to an agreement and we purchased the two sites. I was quite happy with the outcome because not only did we get the control tower, but we also gained two more chicken sites! And although the huts on the airfield were designed for poultry, we decided to turn them into turkey houses and so we began to rear turkeys alongside our chicken business. These two sheds had a full capacity of 40,000 turkeys, on both sites. After the completion of the transaction, the first thing we did was to fix up the control tower. We put railings all round the balcony and on the roof top and renewed its condition. I was very satisfied with the building whilst we were renovating it and I often thought back to when I had watched the Lancasters taking off, as a lad back in the 1940s, but back then I never imagined that I would actually own the control tower one day!

I haven't mentioned that in Lincolnshire, during the late 1960s and early 1970s, they were taking up all the old runways, perimeter tracks and dispersal points to crush the stone, in order to make new motorways. I used to wonder if there would be anything left of these Second World War airfields and think that it was such a shame that there was going to be so little left as a reminder of what those young lads did and sacrificed for the freedom of their country. I remember saying to Harold, one day whilst we were riding across East Kirkby Airfield, that if ever the control tower came up for sale, then we should see if we could buy it, to make sure that it would never be knocked down or destroyed. Fortunately, as you now know, it did come up for sale in 1981 and luckily we happened to be in a situation which allowed us to buy it. That's thanks to Den Brown for letting us know that it was for sale.

Then, in late 1982, a pleasant surprise occurred. A letter arrived informing me that Lord Lilford was willing to sell the Lancaster bomber if we were still interested and it asked us to get in contact with him as soon as possible. Of course we were still interested; very much so! But at the same time I knew that this was going to be one of the hardest decisions of my life. You see, I'd missed the Halifax bomber in 1949 because Father wouldn't allow it. I'd missed the Lancaster in the auction at Squires Gate in 1972 when it came up for auction. I knew now that the time had come that I would have to put my right foot forward! I knew there were going to be several interested clients who were also looking and the chances of it going to America were pretty great.

The Lancaster was based at RAF Scampton at the time, which was only twenty nine miles across country from East Kirkby, so once again we started having to negotiate prices with Lord Lilford's agent, Mr Bracewell and the negotiations took quite a while to be acceptable to both parties, but, eventually, the price was finalised. I am not prepared to say what it did cost, but as I said, it was the hardest decision of my life, because I knew that it was going to all be dead money. I recall saying at the end of the meeting, "I never, ever want to have to make another decision like as long as I live!" But I can confidently tell you today that it was the best decision of the whole of my life; not counting my good wife Betty of course! However, we weren't at the end when we had bought the Lancaster, we then had to move it from RAF Scampton to East Kirkby Airfield, which would create another big expense. What's more, before we could have it dismantled and brought to East Kirkby, we had to have a new hangar put up on the old T2 hangar base, to make sure that it was safely undercover, not far from the control tower and this, of course, was going to incur yet more expense. The purchase of "Just Jane", the Lancaster, was completed in September 1983, but we left it at RAF Scampton for another four years until we built the hangar especially for it. So knowing that we should have this hangar built for 1987, I suddenly wondered whether we could get some help from the Royal Air Force to dismantle and move the Lancaster to East Kirkby. You see it had been the gate guardian at Scampton for 10 years, up to 1983 and then a further four years when we left her there. I went to see the Commanding Officer to acquire some help from the Royal Air Force in dismantling and moving the Lancaster to East Kirkby. At first, they seemed a bit reluctant, but when they knew where she was going and what she was going to stand for, a memorial to Bomber Command and the Second World War, they looked at the project very favourably.

In 1987, the plans were to negotiate terms with RAF Abbington to do the job. RAF Abbington looked at it and assessed the workload, and estimated it would take eleven men thirteen weeks to dismantle, bring to East Kirkby Airfield and put back together again. There were ten lorry loads in all; seven big artic loads and three ordinary lorries. From starting in 1972, when I first became interested in purchasing the Lancaster, then missing it in the auction, buying it in 1983, then moving it in 1987 from Scampton and bringing it to East Kirkby, took a total of fifteen years. I would like to tell you now, that when the very last load of the Lancaster arrived at East Kirkby, complete with a police escort, the job had been completed. Throughout the whole experience, the only time that I got a little emotional about it was when I had a friend with me, called John Chatterton. John had been a Lancaster pilot who had completed his tour of operations over Germany and, not only was he flying during the same period as my brother, he and John were on the same Nuremberg raid during March 1944, John in a Lancaster and Chris in a Halifax. John had also lived at Old Bolingbroke at the same time as us; we lived at the top of the hill, while he lived at the bottom, and he was flying Lancasters while Chris was flying Halifaxes. I'd also like to share with you that when we compared logbooks for the records on the Nuremberg raid, it turned out that there was only one minute's difference between them over Nuremberg. So, as I was saying, the only time I got a little emotional during this process was when I was standing with my friend and I said to him, "We've done it John. We've done it and the RAF has done the job for me." It took a full fifteen years, but during that time, I stayed on a straight road; I never wavered from start to finish.

As I look back at the whole adventure, although I had many frustrations on the journey, I can see that they were all blessings in disguise. If I had bought the Lancaster back in 1973, then I would have taken it straight to the farm and I wouldn't have bought the land on the airfield, which means that I wouldn't have started the Museum and I don't think that our poultry business would have progressed to the level that it is today. So I can see that it was all meant to be. It worked out perfectly!

I just want to say that one week after it had been completed, I went to the Lincolnshire agricultural show and I was walking round the exhibits, when a gentleman on the other side of the roadway just called across when he saw me and said, "You've done it Fred! We never thought you could, but you did ... and you're still married!" I walked across to him and I said, "I'll tell you now, no Lancaster bomber would ever stand between my wife and me." The very next day, whilst I was at East Kirkby, I was so surprised at what another gentleman said to me, because he echoed almost exactly the same words as the gentleman the day before, "You've done it Fred! I never believed you would, but you did and you've still got your health."

Now, there's just one more important thing that I would like to say. When the decision was made to buy the Lancaster and the control tower, the original plan was to purchase them both and have them together on the airfield, with the Lancaster undercover, just across the way from the tower. Harold and I would go and have a look at them when we felt like it, and that was as far as we had thought it out. However, after we had had 'Jane' moved from Scampton to East Kirkby, I went to see the Commanding Officer who asked to see me again. He said to me, "You know Fred, you can't just buy that Lancaster, put it in a building and shut the doors, with no-one else allowed to see it. Everybody should be allowed to see that plane for what it did; it's British history." Of course, once he had said that, it was obvious to both Harold and me that he was right and we had to give everyone the opportunity to see just what the Lancaster and her crews had achieved during The Second World War and what an important part they had played in Britain's history.

But how could we do it? Harold and I talked and talked and discussed our ideas with various interested people and eventually that one comment from the Scampton Commanding Officer led to the creation of our aviation museum in 1987.

At that stage, apart from 'Just Jane' and the Control Tower, there was very little to see at the East Kirby airfield, so we started collecting other exhibits, starting off by purchasing original bomb trailers, David Brown and Ford Standard tractors, which were used for pulling the Lancasters and we gathered all kinds of memorabilia which were connected with aviation and the Second World War. Then, after cleaning and tidying the whole area of the museum, we started putting together cabinets for display and developing the control tower; putting in mannequins and recreating how it would have looked during its years of operation. We developed all the buildings within the museum right up to 1988 and, in 1989, we got to the stage where we could begin to welcome visitors. We had the museum officially opened by the Marshall of the Royal Air Force, Sir Michael Beetham, in August 1989. My wife, Betty, and Harold's wife, Lucy, came to help, particularly looking after the Naafi and the souvenir shop. Visitors started to come in and we continued building the museum up, expanding and developing, which kept us very busy.

Lancaster Bomber 'City of Lincoln' salutes 'Just Jane'

Fred and Betty in the souvenir shop

Chapter Sixteen

A Passion for Fine Craftsmanship

Farm Harvest Wagons

Allow me to leave the Aviation Museum for a time. I haven't mentioned that before we bought the Lancaster, I had a hobby. I had a great interest in old farm wagons, which I used to buy from different local farmers, then renovate and paint them up. I started collecting these old farm wagons in 1976 and the very first one that I bought was what they called the 'Lincolnshire blue spindle-sided wagon', which was built in 1781 and I think I'm right in saying that it's one of the oldest wagons left in Lincolnshire. When you see a Lincolnshire blue spindle-sided wagon and you can see all the craftsmanship and work that's gone into building it, the mind boggles, because the men that built them all those years ago didn't have modern machinery; it was all done by hard hand and muscle labour and craft. To see how they built the wheels and the axles, everything from wood, is amazing. Building a wagon wheel is the most complicated job within joinery and the old hands that used to build them told me, "If you can build a wagon wheel, you can make anything."

I became very interested in these old farm wagons and, up to purchasing the Lancaster, I had ended up with thirty two wagons, all from different counties. You see each county had a different design and colour; they all varied but they were all marvellous things. So we had thirty two, when an opportunity arose to buy what they called a 'Park Drag', or a 'Stage Coach', as you're more likely to know it. It had 'Four-in-hand-driving', which simply meant that it was pulled by four horses. It was built in 1860 and was in very good condition, having actually done very little work. I treasured it because of all the workmanship that had gone into creating it. It was built by Shanks of London, who really were the elite in coach building. My ambition was to have four horses and to have lessons for 'four in hand driving', so we arranged to have these lessons at a place called Darley Dale in Derbyshire. Caroline Dale was my tutor and she was very experienced at 'four-in-hand'. Every now and then, Caroline would come at the weekend with her four horses to give the family a ride in the coach around the local area. So as time went by, I had stables made for five horses, with sufficient grassland for them and eventually the time came when I was ready to begin looking for a team of horses of my own. But then, in 1983, out of the blue, the Lancaster bomber came up for sale again and of course that was it for me. All my old interest flooded back and I knew my heart was with the Lancaster and, as you know, we bought it that year from The Right Honourable Lord Lilford. From then on, from getting the Lancaster and acquiring East Kirkby Airfield and the Control Tower, I never had any time for my wagons and stage coach, because I knew that if I missed the Lancaster now, there would never be another chance to purchase one again. So I turned all my interests into establishing the Lancaster and the Museum as a whole.

I have come to the conclusion that there is only enough time in this life to devote yourself properly to one hobby, so in 1987, I decided to sell all the barn wagons and the stage coach. I have, however, kept three of my best wagons, which are now at my museum at East Kirkby, because they were used during the War years whilst the Lancasters were actually flying. That's the reason I kept them and display them, because they fit in with the Second World War. I do, though, very much regret selling my stage coach; I should have kept it, because it was in such first class, beautiful condition. But there are three wagons in the hanger, near the Lancaster and I do walk past them every day, have a good look at them and give them a little pat. I still admire the craftsmanship that the men had in those days.

So we will now conclude my story of the farm wagons. I do have so much more that I should love to share with you about them, but I shall leave it here, I think.

Fred with his stage coach and horses

Chapter Seventeen

"Just Jane" comes back to Life

Now, back to the Museum and we're in 1990. The museum's coming on, in leaps and bounds with more and more exhibitions. We have managed to find what they call the old 'Queen Mary', which was a vehicle used to transport aircraft back and forth, particularly when any aircraft had crashed. The reason it was called 'Queen Mary' was because it had been named after the Queen Mary, the large ship; so it was named that because of its very large size. They were 60ft long, from nose to tail and during the war years that was a very big lorry to be driving on narrow country roads. It took seven Queen Mary vehicles to transport a Lancaster once it had been dismantled.

So it has come to be very useful, because we now take people for a ride in it, in the back of the trailer. We take them on a journey round the old perimeter track, which is nearly four miles on the airfield, so that they can get some idea of what a bomber airfield looked like during the Second World War. When we first did this, I would usually go on a couple of rounds in an afternoon with different groups and I would stop at certain points of the circuit where I would sit between the trailer and cabin and tell the group my stories and information about that particular part of the perimeter track during the war.

I can confidently say that the attendance is up in numbers every year since opening, which we are very pleased with. It keeps Harold and me very, very busy! We keep adding more staff to our team of workers as we grow. When we started this museum, I said to my brother that if we were going to run a museum then it has to stand on its own two feet and up to now it has done and this is the way we want it to continue. All our staff are paid full rates and we're open six days from Monday to Saturday and we close on Sundays. The only time that I will open on a Sunday is on squadron reunions, for all the squadrons who flew from East Kirkby Airfield. It's very rare that I will open any further Sundays during the year.

Having the museum is so interesting and stimulating, because of the people who come to visit. There are hundreds of veterans from different squadrons, even from other countries; Australia, Germany, America, France, New Zealand, all over the World. Younger generations come taking an interest, families of veterans, people coming and wanting to look at the

Lancaster and control tower. We get schools visiting, students, the media, the young forces' families; it's just amazing.

When we first opened the museum, there were two miners who would come from Derby every week and just sit on chairs in the hangar all day, just sit and look at the Lancaster. They came every week, year in, year out. When they had been coming for several weeks, one of them, named Bill, said to me, "Wouldn't it be lovely to start one of the engines on the Lancaster?" And nearly every week after he had first said it, he would say the same thing, "Wouldn't it be lovely to start one of the engines on the Lancaster, just one?" I would say to him, "It would Bill", but I never thought for one minute at the time that we would eventually get them up and running.

This had been going on from 1989 up to 1994 and at the beginning of 1994 I was starting to think that maybe we ought to get one of the engines running, but whilst I used to run this through my mind, "One day, we probably will get one started," I also knew that the engines hadn't been running since 1971 and now it was 1994. That's twenty three years since the engines had been run, so I knew that was going to be a major operation, even to attempt to get one started.

I'd been thinking about it for several weeks, when one day a gentleman came to the museum and whilst he was at the pay desk he asked, "Is there a Mr Fred Panton around?" So they sent somebody across to fetch me from the hangar to come and see the gentleman. He said to me, "I've just called in Mr Panton, because I've heard that you're thinking of starting one of the engines up on the Lancaster." "That's right," I replied, but I was actually thinking to myself, "I don't think you'll be able to do that!" He told me that he had just come out of the Air Force and had been at RAF Coningsby, working on the Battle of Britain Flight as an engineer on the Battle of Britain Lancaster. He asked me if I was interested in trying to start one of the engines, then could I give him the job to do it? He wanted to come and have a look and to do the job. So, after talking to him for a while, I agreed that he could come and have a look at the engines, to see what he thought and see how big a job it would be to make one start. The arrangement was for him to come the following Monday morning to examine one of the engines. However, in the meantime, I rang RAF Coningsby, Battle of Britain Flight to speak to the Chief Engineer there, whose name was Flight Lieutenant Barry Sears. I rang because I wanted to ask him if he knew a man called Ian Hickling, which was the name of the gentleman who had come to see me. He was able to confirm everything that Ian had said about coming from the Battle of Britain Flight. So I asked him, "Is he capable of starting one of the engines up on our Lancaster?" and you know, he said to me, "He most certainly is Fred." So that was it; I engaged him to do the job to see if it was possible to try and start the engine.

Ian came on the Monday morning with his tools and overalls and we soon realised that we were going to have to have something to get up to the engines of the Lancaster, because they're about 18ft from the ground. I arranged to have a tractor and hydraulic tipping trailer to lift Ian up to get level with the engines, so that he had plenty of room to work. We decided to try and start number three engine, which is on the right hand side of the pilot's seat. Ian started to take the plug stoppers out to take any compression off the engines, so that if the props would turn then they would turn easily. After taking all the plug stoppers out, he proceeded to take hold of one of the propellers and pull it downwards to see if all the pistons would move. To our very pleasant surprise, and it was a big surprise for Ian, the twelve pistons all started to move up and down, which was the first time they'd done that for twenty three years. Ian could hardly believe it! He went on to do further investigations of parts of the engine and was very satisfied with what he saw, so he announced to me that it was possible to get the engine up and running. He was so pleased with what he had seen of the first engine that he said that he would just love to see if the other engines were in as good condition as number three. So we decided to look at number four engine. Again, he took all the plug stoppers out to take the compression off and proceeded to turn the prop as he had done before and to our amazement all twelve pistons started to go up and down. So we resolved to give engines one and two a test as well, to see if the engines were all the same. We went through all the same processes with the plug stoppers and turning the props and, astonishingly, both one and two piston-ends started moving. After twenty three years they were all still working beautifully, it was amazing. So, because of the quality of her condition, we decided to start straight away to try and get number three engine running, because it contained all the hydraulics. The very next day, Ian was given the go-ahead to get started. Now, Ian had a very good friend, Roy Jarman, who was another engineer with whom he had worked for quite a number of years and Ian said that he would like him to come to help to get the first engine running. I agreed to that straight away and said to him, "If that's what you want, that'll be all right Ian."

The first job was to take the propellers off the engine, then take parts of the engine to pieces. Next, the radiator came off, followed by all the electrics. The camshafts were checked, the props rebalanced and all the rubber seals and piping had to be renewed. There was a lot of work to be done, not just on the engine, but all the wiring and the instruments in the cockpit had to be checked and renewed where necessary. Even the pressure gauges and all the petrol tanks had to be thoroughly tested. But to cut a long story short, it took those two men four months to complete the job, a total of 1,250 man hours, just for one engine!

Eventually, after much work, the time came when we were ready to press the button to see if our first engine would start. We had to acquire some Avgas petrol, which had a high, 100 octane, lead content, which was the same petrol as they used with the Lancasters during the war. There are six petrol tanks on a Lancaster bomber, three tanks per wing, with a total capacity of just over two thousand gallons. However, just to see if the first engine would start, we only used fifty gallons in one tank. You see, our biggest problem wasn't actually starting the engine, but because it had been such a long time since it had last been started, we had to make sure that there wasn't going to be a fire; this was our greatest danger. So to make absolutely sure this wouldn't happen we had the local fire engine down with five men all ready, just in case. Then, the $64,000 question was about to be answered! Ian climbed into the Lancaster fuselage by walking up the steps, making his way to the cockpit and to the Flight Engineer's seat, ready to press the starter buttons. I knew for a fact that he was very nervous and a little bit trembley; the time had come to prove himself. He pressed the button and the props started to turn very slowly, but it just didn't start immediately because it had got an air-lock, understandably after standing all those years. After sorting that out we started again. Ian pressed the button for a second time and the props started to go round. They went round about six times and then there was a cough from the engine and a puff of smoke. Two more coughs sounded, followed by another two puffs of smoke and then, suddenly, it started up! It was wonderful to see the look of excitement on the faces of the firemen and the people gathered round when they saw that engine start after 23 years! Ian ran the engine for the first time for just three quarters of a minute, then stopped it and gave the engine a good checking over. We ran her up to between 700 and 800 revs a minute, until we could gradually build them up to 2500 revs within three weeks.

So after all the excitement of starting the first engine, we decided that we really should try another one. We agreed upon number two engine and we went through all the same processes again, which again took four months to complete, the same as the first job had taken. The time came to see if number two would start, and she performed exactly the same as number one had. At the time, I remember the thought going through my head that it was like nurturing a baby into walking, one step at a time. We had to build it up to 2500 revs, the maximum that we would go to. However the absolute maximum revs that a Lancaster bomber could reach was 3000 flat out. Getting the second engine running to perfection gave us the incentive to continue onto the next engine and we went to number four engine, which, again, took us four months to complete. We reached 2000 revs successfully and so it was a given that we would go the full hog and start number one engine. All in all, it took us sixteen months to get all four engines running and for the last two engines, it had been twenty three years since they had last been started. This takes us to 1995 and, at last, we had a Lancaster with all four engines fully operational.

After a time we decided that we would like to try and get, "Just Jane", it to taxiing condition, to run under her own power. To get to this condition, we had to look at the hydraulic system and the brakes, which took a further six weeks. Eventually the time came when we could try taxiing the Lancaster and letting her run on her own and this was going to be a big day! The pilot we had chosen to do this was the son of my good friend Flight Pilot Officer John Chatterton, Lieutenant Mike Chatterton, who was flying Lancasters with the Battle of Britain flight, so he was well up to date. The day came to put all of our work and planning into action. Ian and Mike climbed into the Lancaster and took their positions to start the engines. Roy had pumped the petrol through the systems, the engines were started up, chocks were pulled away and we were ready to eat the proof of our pudding!

Mike put his hand up, signalling all ready for the go. Then, he gave the engines a small rev, let the brakes off and she started to pull away, all under her own power. This was the first time for over twenty three years and seeing all four engines running, really was the most emotional thing to me and I will admit that sight did make me shed a tear or two, to see her moving so majestically.

During sixteen months of renovating and re-doing the engines, there were many changes and advancements within the museum and the attendance of customers visiting us was steadily growing to our satisfaction.

People were hearing about what we were doing and the museum was gaining steady public interest. I'd like to come back to the development of the Lancaster and the museum a bit later.

Success at last!

Chapter Eighteen

Back to Visit Beloved Osberton

For now, I'd like to tell you about one gentleman who came to the museum and who stirred a very great interest within me. This person came to the museum and he made his acquaintance with me. He came and asked me if I was Mr Panton and he said to me, "I gather you used to live at Osberton Estate near Worksop?" and I said, "That's right, I did. My father lived as a rabbit catcher / game keeper." He told me that he lived on the Osberton Estate, which of course I was very eager to hear about. I was so pleased to meet someone who had come from Osberton. Then I told him that we had lived there from 1939 to 1942, up to the airfield being built, after which time we came back to Lincolnshire. When he mentioned my beautiful Osberton Estate, I told him, "It was one of the most beautiful places I have ever lived in my life. I went to school there, in Scofton village and ever since we left, I have never failed to go back and visit once or twice every year. I never miss a chance to revisit my memories of the place that influenced me so much, and in truth still does. That's how much of an impression that lovely Estate left on me." I can tell you, as soon as he first mentioned it, time meant nothing to me, I just wanted to know more and more about Osberton because I have such wonderful memories of it. While we were reminiscing and talking he told me that he shoots pheasants a few days each year, on the Osberton Estate, which I found to be of great interest. I told him that I did quite a lot of pheasant shooting myself and I asked if it would be possible for me to get a day's shooting on the Osberton Estate. You see, when we lived there, it would be unheard of for someone like me to shoot on the Estate. In the days when my father was a keeper there, it was all very private. There would be no paying guests, it would be only Dukes, friends and Lords; it was a game for the hierarchy, which we respected very much. So he said, "Leave it with me and I'll see what I can do for you." Now, it wasn't long before he contacted me to tell me that he had arranged for me to go and have a day's shooting on the Estate. You cannot believe how I felt when I was given that chance to go and have a day at that place I loved so much and, of course, I started to think and go back. I wondered what my father would have thought about me going to do that? During my father's game-keeping days, every acre of the Estate was very heavily guarded by keepers, so much so, that I started feeling nervous just to think that I was going shooting on that estate!

So the day eventually arrived to go and our meeting point was at the old school in Scofton village which I used to attend as a young lad. It's closed now, but the school is still there and it's exactly the same as it was. It has never been touched or added to; it's still the same as I remember in 1938. The only difference is that they've made it into one big room, whereas there used to be a big room partition to separate the classes. The windows and doors are still the same and I could mark the spot within twelve inches of where my desk was when I used to sit in that classroom. But the most marvellous part of it all is that hanging on the outside wall is the old bell which we used to ring from the inside, and it's still very much still intact and in working order. When I arrived that morning at the school, Captain Foljambe, who the estate belongs to, came to welcome us, and I told him that I used to go to school here for nearly four years and how amazed I was that the original bell, from before 1938, is still on the wall. It must be years and years and years since it was last rung, and when I told Captain Foljambe the story he said to me, "Well, I'll untie the rope and let you ring the bell." It rang and it sounded exactly the same as it had to me back in 1938. To me, to be able to ring that bell was unbelievable. The nostalgia was overpowering and it took me right back to my school days.

After this we started our day and, as we were driving around the estate, I could remember back to the days of my childhood and I knew exactly where we were and where I'd been with my father. I'm sure that that one day of shooting and thinking about all the different places that I had been with him, was the equivalent of having a whole month's holiday somewhere else. Since that day of shooting I must have been accepted as a safe shot, because I now go every year for several days shooting, which I enjoy doing very much. It is the highlight of my year going back to Osberton and long may it continue.

Going back to the Museum again and we're still developing. Our visitor numbers are growing monthly, and we're starting to get schools coming from different areas, we're attracting people from abroad and we're having war veterans from different squadrons coming to have their yearly reunions. People are coming to see the engine taxi runs and we've started introducing night runs for the Lancaster, to make the effect more authentic and dramatic, which draws very large crowds, so we currently do this twice a year. We have also started hosting a 1940s dance once a year in the hangar, which attracts between five hundred and six hundred people. Our full-time staff consists of around fifteen, but our numbers are growing every year. We occasionally take the Lancaster on the thirty five acre grass field to taxi, which makes everything look so real, just as it would have done during the war years. We have started doing corporate days where we take bookings for groups who have a tour inside the Lancaster, a taxi ride and have a meal with us.

All this kept Harold and me occupied, taking us to 1999, by which time my two sons, David and Phillip, were running and expanding the poultry and my grandson, James, had also joined the poultry side of our business. David had decided to put up a large new poultry unit for the broiler chickens which has a capacity of 300,000 broiler chickens, which will produce 2,100,000 yearly. We have one of the most up-to-date poultry sites in Europe and it's completely computerised, which means that we know exactly how much water the chickens have drunk in twenty four hours, how much food they have eaten and how much gas the sheds have consumed each day to keep the temperature up. The technology allows the sheds to control the temperatures independently, the atmosphere and the air-intake to keep the birds healthy and clean. So, as you can see, it's one of the most advanced poultry sites ever to have been developed and it is working very well for us. All our sites are very efficient and top quality with very high standards.

We now needed a convoy of feed lorries

The start of a wonderful day at Osberton with Richard, Fred's son in law

Fred and Betty go back to Scofton village school

Chapter Nineteen

My Hunt for Nielsen Continues

Now, I would like to divert you back to Chris Nielsen once more. I had said earlier, how much I wished to find him again, to try and make contact with him, but all my efforts came to no avail. However, one day at the end of October 1999, an American man and wife visited the museum. They arrived in the morning and were there all day up until half an hour before closing time at 4.00pm. Now, just before this, the American went into the Naafi and asked one of the assistants if there was a Mr Panton around. I came to meet this gentleman in the Naafi, where we have a model of my brother's aircraft hanging from the ceiling. It's a replica of the one he was shot down in and the squadron letters on this model are "BMN", which was for 433 squadron, Skipton-on-Swale, North Yorkshire. The 'N' stood for 'Nuts'.

The ground crew who used to look after the plane and keep it serviced, christened it and wrote in large letters, "Nielsen's Nut House" after the pilot, Chris Nielsen, on the nose of the Halifax. This gentleman wanted to know who Nielsen was. I told him that it stood for 'Nielsen's Nut House, pilot officer Christian Nielsen' and he said to me, "My father was in partnership with a Christian Nielsen." Of course, this turned out to be the very same Nielsen and he told me that the Nielsens were family friends. I said that I wished I'd known him ten years ago and explained my twelve year search for Nielsen. He then told me that during all the years they had known him, they had never had any idea that he had flown with the Canadian Air Force; he had never mentioned it once. He was so pleased to discover some of the history of his friend and to meet the brother of his flight engineer. He didn't know anything at all about the history of Nielsen's flying days and so he was very interested to find somebody who could put the picture of Nielsen's history together for him. He then proceeded to call his mother, over in America, on his mobile phone then and there, to tell her that he had met the brother of Chris Nielsen's flight engineer.

After his phone call to his mother, he told me that Chris Nielsen had died a few years ago and that his wife had died one year ago. He did say, though, that they were very big family friends, so, straight away, I asked him, "Would it be possible to find out if Chris Nielsen still had his uniform, or any photographs of when he was flying, to put in the museum, because I should love to get hold of anything like that, with his being my brother's pilot."

"Leave it with me and I'll see what I can do," he replied.

Anyway, when he got back home to America about three weeks later, I received a letter from him to say that he had made enquiries, but just before Nielsen's wife died, she gave his uniform, medals and wartime log that he had kept during his time in the prisoner of war camp, to a youth in town. He also told me that the sad part of it all is this young lad has been seen walking round town in the uniform. He continued to say that all is not lost because he was going to see if they could find this youth to try and get it back again for me. So I was hoping and keeping my fingers crossed as time went by. Six weeks later I received another letter explaining that they couldn't find this youth and their search had been fruitless. So that was more or less the end of the story. When I got that letter my heart seemed to stop a beat or two, thinking "Well, that is it."

I'll continue with this story, but to do so I'm going to have to jump forward a bit. Two years after receiving that letter from the American gentleman, I went into my office in the Naafi one Saturday morning, just after the postman had been and found on my desk, a letter addressed to Mr F Panton and marked 'Private'. I opened the letter and found that it was from a young lad in Wales and there were four pages, hand written. We were very busy at the museum and we had a big day in front of us with a lot of people expected. I was wanted here, there and everywhere! I said to myself, that I didn't have time to read all that then, I should have to read it when I got a chance later. Eventually, when I did get the time to read it, it was the following Tuesday and I ended up wishing that I'd read it straight away, because this twenty year old lad was wanting to know if I was the brother of a Flight Engineer Christopher Whitton Panton? He had just purchased a Canadian uniform from a clothing shop in America and when he received it, not only did he get the uniform, but also the wartime log and medals with it. He said that it belonged to a Pilot Officer Christian Nielsen and he'd been looking through the log, this diary, where Nielsen had written all the names of his crew, including the name of Flight Engineer Chris Panton. I just couldn't believe what I was reading. But the trouble was that he'd never given his telephone number in the letter and I was so excited about the information that I couldn't wait to be writing and waiting for answers, I had to ring him and tell him that I was the brother of Chris Panton. So I started to try and find his telephone number in Wales. It took me at least half a day to get hold of it and when I did, at about 4 o'clock in the afternoon, his mother answered. So I told her who I was, Fred Panton and that I had received this letter from her son and he wanted to know if I was the brother of Christopher Panton, which, of course, I told her I was and she seemed very excited that I had rung her and given her this information. They called her son Richard Bonney and she told me that Richard was at work at a big store and wouldn't be home until 10 o'clock at night; I believe they were repricing all their goods. She also told me that every time he came home at night, his first question was, "Is there a letter from Mr Panton?" and now I had rung for him, she would ring him to see if he could come home early to speak to me. He would be very happy and excited to get this information and he would ring me as soon as he got home from work, so of course I gave her my telephone number. After a few hours, Richard arrived home after being fetched and gave me a ring. "Mr Panton?" I said "Yes?" "I'm Richard Bonney, thank you for contacting me," to which I replied, "I find it very hard to believe that you've got my brother's pilot's uniform. Where did you come to get this uniform, because I've been trying to find Chris Nielsen for over twelve years?" So he told me how he acquired it and after talking with him for a while, he told me he would send some photographs of the uniform, the medals and the diary. So that was it and I was waiting anxiously to receive these photographs. We also arranged that he would come one Saturday to let me have a look at the uniform, which would be three weeks from our telephone call.

I would like to tell you at this point how he had come to get this uniform. He had been sitting in his house one day when he just thought to himself, "I'll just have a browse on the internet," and he eventually happened to find this clothes shop in America where they were going to be having a sale. In this sale there was going to be a pilot officer's uniform, but it never mentioned medals or a wartime diary in the description. Richard told me that he is very interested in wartime memorabilia, so when he saw it for sale he was determined to try and buy it when it came up in the auction by bidding on the telephone. However, the day it was due to come up for availability he was rushed into hospital with appendicitis, so nothing was done. However, when he came out of hospital from his operation, he was sitting in the house recuperating when he thought to himself that he would check to see if the officer's uniform had been sold. He rang them up and they told him they still had the uniform available, so he said to his Father, "I want this uniform, Dad, can you ring them up and give them a price?" His

Father didn't want to do it, but he begged and begged him and after quite a while he persuaded him to put an offer in. So eventually they bought it and it was delivered to them in Wales and of course they found it to be my brother's pilot's uniform; the very thing that I wanted. When he told me that story I was absolutely convinced that I was going to have it and I said to Harold, "I'll have that uniform!" and he said, "He'll never, ever part with that uniform, Fred." I said, "He most *certainly* will, this is *no* coincidence. We shall see!"

The Saturday came for him to visit and bring the uniform for me to have a look at. He came with his mother and father and I remember that we were very busy at the museum that particular day. He was looking for me from when he arrived and I had been keeping my eye open for him all morning, because we hadn't arranged an arrival time. We eventually met in the doorway of the Naafi. Richard said, "Fred Panton?" and we went from there. After making our acquaintance and having a cup of tea together, he informed me that he had left the uniform on the back seat of his car until he met me and all this time I was thinking, "I'm going to tell him that I want that uniform," but I couldn't just do it straight away, I had to wait for the right time and place to say it. So I walked him and his parents round the museum, and I took them to have a look at the Lancaster and the exhibitions in the control tower. The whole time I was showing him around, I was only thinking about what I was going to say to him; I just could not wait to see that uniform. After showing them round the museum, I took them to the memorial chapel to see all the names of the men who had been killed from the airfield. There are eight hundred and forty names of men from 57 and 630 Squadron, all aircrew who flew from East Kirkby Airfield. That's the equivalent of one hundred and forty seven Lancasters failing to return from operations, all in twenty one months.

After completing the tour of the memorial chapel, I came to the conclusion that the time had come that I was going to tell to him that I wanted that uniform. During the time taking them round the hangar and showing the various buildings and exhibits, I was sensing that his father was a very quiet, very reserved person who made little conversation. So when we were coming out of the memorial chapel I said, "Now Richard, I want to say something to you and I want to say it in front of your father and mother so that they can hear. That uniform you've got, I want it. You'll probably find this difficult to understand, but you see that Lancaster in the hangar? I think a *lot* of that aircraft, but I think *more* of that uniform, because that

146

uniform was part of my brother's history. It was part of my brother's pilot's life and I want it." Now, his father spoke for the first time and he said to me, "We thought you might say that, so we've had it valued," and I said, "Good." We went to my office in the Naafi, all three of us, while Richard went to the car park to fetch the uniform from the boot of his car. We sat down in the office talking while Richard was out. He eventually knocked and came in, carrying the uniform on a coat hanger. He laid it down on my desk and I said to him, "Now Richard, I'm going to say this, again in front of your mother and father; do you realise what you have just done? You've just delivered to me and put on my desk Chris Nielsen's uniform. Richard, you will never, ever do a greater deed as long as you live, as what you've done today. You can come to this museum free of charge, as often as you like, for the rest of your life," and then I said, "How much do you want for it?" His father showed me the valuation for the uniform, the medals and the war-time diary and he told me that Richard hadn't had enough money to buy it himself, so his mother, father and another member of his family had all had to give him some money in order to buy it. Then he told me how much he wanted for it. I can't tell you the price for it, but I said to him, "Is that what you want?" When he said "Yes," I burst out with absolute passion and determination, "I'll *have* it!" I couldn't give him the money fast enough.

So, after receiving the uniform, at the end of the day when everyone had gone home, I stood looking at the uniform laid out on the back of my chair, in my house. I thought to myself of all the 12 to 14 years I'd been trying to find my brother's pilot and somehow or other, it had been done by a twenty year old student living in Wales.

I don't mind in the slightest what anyone thinks, that has *got* to be divine intervention. As far as I'm concerned that is a miracle. I don't mind whether you believe or accept that or not, but to me it's true in my heart, because I had given up all hope of finding any connections to my brother's pilot. I would also like to mention, just before I finish, that I now have in my possession, my brother's wireless operator's uniform. Pilot Officer H. Cooper gave it to me while I was visiting him in Vancouver. I have also, as you now know, pilot officer Christian Nielsen's uniform. The reason I am telling you this, is that once a year we have a 1940s dance at the museum, as I previously mentioned and I occasionally let two of my grandsons wear these uniforms for this night. It's the only night they are allowed to be worn, but my grandson, Andrew Panton, will wear Nielsen's uniform and one of my other grandsons, Robert Myers, will wear Cooper's. You would think that they had been tailor-made for each of them; they fit beautifully and as they're walking around and dancing on this night, it's uncanny; I can clearly see my brother's crew.

Monty Thompson who worked alongside Fred and Harold literally all day and all night – until 2pm the following day, without a grumble, to ensure the ex-RAF buildings were erected and fit to house a huge consignment of chickens. Even now, whenever Fred and Monty meet, their first words are always, "Do you remember it?"

Well done Mont!

(See Chapter 11)

Chapter Twenty

Exceeding Expectations

Going back some time to the early days of the museum for a moment, I would like to tell you of another fortunate opportunity that arose for my wife and me. I had always wondered what it would be like to live in a large house on an estate with parkland, with it being part of my history in quite a large way. The opportunity actually came in 1989, at a place called Tumby Lawn. The timing seemed to be right because my youngest son, David, was taking more responsibility in the poultry enterprise and was starting to want a bigger house for his family, so Betty and I moved to Tumby Lawn. I must say that it was a very grand old mansion, where we enjoyed living very much. The estate itself belonged to Sir David Hawley and I leased the residence from him for an agreed number of years. Another attraction about the estate was that it also had a very good pheasant shoot which I had the pleasure of shooting on for several years. I can say with fond memories that Betty and I enjoyed every day that we lived there.

Back to the mid-nineties at the museum, the media were starting to take an active interest in us now and various film productions were coming to use the Lancaster and her surroundings for their footage. Harold and I are pleased and proud of the museum's achievements and development. It really has exceeded our expectations. We have been open quite a number of years now and we have, over time, put together three videos, the first being 'Two farmers and a Lancaster,' the second being 'Operation Lancaster' and the third is 'Just Jane'. These are all still available and as popular as ever, and they tell the story of the museum, it's history, and all our stories about the actors and VIPs who have visited over the years and all manner of interesting things. The most recent adventure with the media was in July 2007, when we hosted the Antiques Roadshow, which proved to be a very great success. I'd like to mention some notable figures who we have had the honour of having visit us over time. They include: The Duke of Gloucester, actor Sir Richard Todd, on several occasions, actor Christopher Plummer, from the Sound Of Music, actor Stephen Fry, Fred Dibnah and Sir Michael Beetham, who was Marshall of the Royal Air Force, Raymond Baxter, the author and commentator, Sir David Frost, the BBC interviewer, and Squadron Leader John Willis, who later became Marshall of the Royal Airforce. We've also entertained Les Monroe, the 617 Squadron Pilot

Officer on the Dambusters raid, Bill Reed, who is another bomber pilot, Sir Leonard Cheshire and his wife, Sue Ryder and even Rosemary Chadwick, the daughter of Roy Chadwick, who actually designed the Lancaster Bomber. This long list does not even include the many television presenters such as Judith Chalmers, John Craven, the Country File presenter, Michael Aspel, the Antiques Road Show presenter, News Reader, Sophie Rayworth and the Irish country singer Mary Duff and 'Just Jane' herself, Cristobel Leighton-Porter! Only a few mentioned from a list of many others

Now, I'd also like to tell you about a very unexpected honour in my life, which I'm very proud of. In November 2002, whilst living at Tumby Lawn, I had a great surprise when I received a letter from 10, Downing Street informing me that my name was being put forward for consideration for receiving an MBE award. This came as a great shock, but a very welcome and pleasant surprise! The Prime Minister wanted to know if it would be agreeable to me, before my name was officially put forward to Her Majesty. The letter went on to read that they would be grateful if I could notify them by return of post, and of course, I accepted very gladly. So, on New Year's Day 2003, I was on the New Year's Honours list to receive an MBE. This made me feel very humble; the thoughts going through my head were very much along the lines of, "Why me?" because you don't do any of this work to receive an award or recognition. You do your work and as you go along you build momentum, but you don't notice it because it feels natural. This said, it is a great honour to be given such an award. It was something I was very pleased to accept and I feel very privileged.

But this wasn't our first trip to Buckingham Palace because three years prior to this I had received an invitation from the Lord Chamberlain for me and Betty, and Harold and his wife Lucy, to attend a garden party at Buckingham Palace in July of 2000. This was quite a surprise and a pleasure to receive and the thoughts I had took me back to my school days, learning about all the previous Kings and Queens of our country. You never dream that you will, one day, be invited to the residence of the Queen of England. To be in her presence and to see her in person is an overwhelming experience and it really confirms how honoured you are being there. But what a fantastic event, to go and see everything in all of its splendour; it makes you very proud to be British and gives you a great feeling of being one of the luckiest on this Earth to experience such grandeur. The highlight of the MBE investiture was when I was presented with the MBE by Prince Charles. I was put at such ease when I walked up to him to accept the award, because he was such a gentleman and, from feeling very nervous, I soon relaxed and felt that I could speak to him all day. I shall never ever forget the day that I met Prince Charles, it was such an honour.

All of this happened between 2000 and 2003 and by now we had been living at Tumby Lawn for nearly sixteen years. Betty and I were starting to get older and it began to cross our minds that we probably ought to be looking for a smaller residence for our more mature years. An opportunity arose when a house came up for sale near Spilsby, very close to where I was born and brought up during my early years. It was a house that seemed to fit the bill for us to settle down in and I actually remember this house being built during the late 1930s. It came up for sale a little sooner than we wanted really, but still, we decided that we would purchase it. So we moved, once again, from Tumby Lawn back to Spilsby in 2004, which was a bit sad because we had enjoyed living at Tumby Lawn very much. Our new residence has made our lives much more manageable now, however, and we both take great pleasure from our gardening here. We are very happy.

Tumby Lawn

Fred receiving his MBE from Prince Charles

Fred and Betty share a proud moment

Chapter Twenty One

Another Mission to Germany

For a long, long time, it had been my desire and ambition to go to Berlin and the chance arose in April of 2009. I went with two friends, Mr Peter Ratcliff and Mr Jim Shortland, who is a historian and an RAF veteran. Jim used to fly in Lancasters during the War and had completed his full tour of operations. We also planned to meet with a German historian, who would be staying with us throughout our stay to show us round and give us all the historical facts about the places that we would visit. The reason I wanted to go to Berlin was because, during the war years, we children knew Berlin as 'The Big City' because it was so heavily guarded and the home to the top brass of Nazi Germany. I went with these two men because they'd been twice before and knew exactly where to find all the interesting places related to the Second World War, including all the living quarters, working offices and so on. It seemed like a golden opportunity to be shown round by three of the best people available. So we flew at 39,000 ft and just over five hundred miles per hour from Stansted Airport direct to Berlin. It took an hour and a half flying time, which seemed like a really long time to me, because I'm not all that keen on flying!

While we were in the air, my mind was going back to the war years when Bomber Command was flying over to bomb Berlin using Lancasters and Halifaxes. When we landed at Berlin airport I was thinking to myself, "However did those Lancasters manage to do it?" My flight seemed like an uncomfortably long time, even at that speed, but the Lancasters and Halifaxes were flying at a lot less than half the speed we were, at only half the height, maybe 18,000 to 20,000 ft. On top of that, they had to turn round again and come straight home after they had done the bombing. It made me appreciate on a deeper level what those boys had to do. You see, as soon as they hit the coast of Europe, there would be guns trying to shoot them down, there'd be all the search lights trying to find them in the sky and night fighters looking for them. It would be a battle all the way from the coast line to Berlin and it would be the same all the way back again. This would have made an approximate total flying time of between eight to nine hours. Not only that, but in those days the chances of a mechanical fault occurring were very great indeed. I soon realised and appreciated what all those young lads did for the freedom of our country and I'm sure that I'm right in saying that a crew had to do thirty missions to complete a tour of operations before they could stand down or rest. To complete thirty missions in those conditions has got to be a miracle. It also dawned on me that what Harold and I had done together at the museum was definitely the right thing to do. Never ever to be forgotten, because there is a saying, you know, "If you don't learn from experience, history will repeat itself."Arriving in Berlin and catching a train from the airport to our hotel in the centre of the city, gave us a chance to see some of Berlin from the train and I was able to see just how clean everything was. The people were so respectful and they had impressively got everything all built up very nicely from the devastation caused during the war years.

We arrived at our hotel at around 2 o'clock in the afternoon and I must say how welcoming the hotel was and the food was second to none. We settled in and then we went to have a sight-seeing cruise on one of the boats on the river. I enjoyed this very much, travelling up the river and seeing all the lovely buildings, not long after being built. You see, nearly 85% of Berlin had been destroyed during the war. We had with us a German interpreter-historian who stayed with us every day of our seven day visit, walking around with us and explaining the history of all the places that we visited. He took us to every place that we wanted to see. On the Sunday morning when I woke up, what amazed me and was so nice to hear were the church bells ringing all over the city, which we rarely hear over here in England, and it seemed so beautiful and peaceful. The sun was shining and it was beautiful weather all week. But to hear all the church bells ringing, it took me back sixty years, to how it used to be in England, when we would ring all our church bells on a Sunday morning and I really enjoyed that.

One particular reason I came to Berlin was to see Hitler's bunker and on the Sunday, our historian guide took us to the place where Hitler's bunker was, which is a car park today. I am to understand that the bunkers are still there, but you can't go inside. I did, however, as our historian pointed out, stand on top of Hitler's bunker, the place where he committed suicide. He pointed out to us where a bomb had been dropped and where they cremated his body after he had committed suicide. The bunkers are quite central in the city, in a nice built up area. They have been built upon, as I said and levelled off so you can't get inside anymore, but they've all been preserved underground and built over with this car park. It covered quite a large area because he was surrounded with guards and large gardens and even though it's all been built upon now, people can still visit and see where it was. We went to see a building where Hermann Goering, head of the Luftwaffe was stationed. The big building containing his offices, which didn't get bombed during the war, stands there now, just as it did when it was first built. Our historian told us that there were twenty five thousand people working in this building during the war, all to do with the Luftwaffe, the German Air Force. It was a big, long building, made of stone and the surprising thing was that it had all been built in one year, which I found amazing. This building was relatively close to the bunkers, in fact all the main offices were fairly tightly knitted together, all within a quarter of a mile radius of each other. We also went to see where Goebbels had lived, which had been bombed during the War. His house was no more than three to four hundred metres from the bunkers and, just as the offices all had to be in close vicinity, so did their homes. The house wasn't anything spectacular at all. It was a very ordinary, fair sized building, which would have been quite new at the time he lived there, because it probably isn't any more than one hundred years old now. It has all been built back up again today, so well that you can't see the seams joining the original to new parts. They kept all the building plans of everything, so that they were able to rebuild and put everything back together again. After that we went to see the offices of Lord Haw-Haw (the British traitor) which were again within walking distance from the bunkers, maybe a mile or so. The main barracks of the SS, where Himmler was stationed, was perhaps half a mile from the bunkers, so really the whole hub of the top Nazi offices and homes were all within a two mile radius of each other. I wouldn't say it was any more than that. You see they all had to be close to one another for meetings and planning and reporting, etc. These were all places that I wanted to see because I had remembered them from during the war. It was the centre where all the evil of the War had been planned and created by these people. Obviously there were offices in Nuremberg and Munich, but the bulk of it had taken place in the centre of Berlin. I found it all very interesting, because I used to hear about it on the news. You know, we all learned a lot about it when we were young and when this happens you find as you get older you naturally want to go and look at the place that was so infamous during those dreadful years.

Later in the week, we went to see the Olympic Stadium, which had been built in 1935, and where Hitler had sat at the 1936 Olympic Games. I was told that it was built to accommodate seventy five thousand people, seated, and you could see the place where he had sat from where we stood. It was a great big building made of stone, needing very little maintenance, which I found very interesting to look at. The car parks, road ways, living quarters and swimming pools for the athletes and the stadium were all built in one year, which is mind-boggling, and yet it still looks as though it was only recently built because it was never bombed. We continued to sight-see for the remainder of the week and I had never realised, but the historian pointed out that there were more bridges in Berlin than any other city in the world. We were also taken to see where Hitler's dentist had worked, where there is still a functioning surgery. It was actually Hitler's dentist who indentified his body after he had committed suicide. We went to Sachsenhausen, which is between thirty five to forty miles outside Berlin, which wasn't a pleasant place to go, but we felt we really should go to look at it. Visiting Sachsenhausen gives you a very funny feeling, a feeling which is very difficult to explain. The camp covers a massive area, and it was one of the biggest concentration camps in Germany. I had previously been to a German concentration camp in Dachau in 1972, so even before we arrived at Sachsenhausen, I had some idea of what we were going to be seeing. Dachau was a very dark place which still held a strong feeling around it of sadness and discomfort. The birds never sing or fly near or around it and the grass and flowers never grow there. It's like dead land. Visiting Sachsenhausen and trying to explain the feelings I had, is about trying to visualise what it must have been like to be living in a country with concentration camps, which were exercising such evil. It makes you wonder how men could bring themselves to commit such terrible atrocities and what is was they were trying to achieve by doing this. It was a very depressing and hopeless atmosphere. It's difficult to put into words, because there's so much passing through your mind. It seems, seeing this place, that they can't have had any consciences, otherwise they could never had committed those terrible crimes on innocent men, women and children. On leaving such a place you end up coming to the conclusion that everything that the British and the allies did in the Second World War *had* to be done to give these people their freedom back. You come to the conclusion that we had been fighting the devil himself.

During the rest of our time there, we were also able to visit the flat towers, which guarded Berlin with the big guns. So we went to all the places where the Nazis were operating during the war years that I had always been interested in seeing. Back in the city, we visited a museum and this museum was a model of Germania, which was designed by Albert Speer, the architect. Hitler was going to have it built if he had won the War and it was going to be the representation of the Capital of the World. The model we visited was about 30ft by 15ft and it showed all the gardens and details. Albert Speer had warned Hitler that if Germania were to be built it would be in the clouds most of the time and it was possible that it could even rain inside. But Hitler would not believe that and he stayed resolute that he would build it, when he won the war. The seating inside was to accommodate one hundred and eighty thousand seated people and it would have been very, very impressive. All the stone that it would have been built with at the time was going to be given to him. I should imagine that the stone would have belonged to one of the big businessmen of Berlin who would have owned one of the stone quarries. A lot of the building that had been done during the War was carried out by slave labour, so, although I don't know for certain, it might have been that Hitler would have planned Germania to have been built using slave labour too. It's also quite possible that Hitler would have just demanded the stone and wouldn't have expected to pay for it, so, just as the architect, Albert Speer, would have been made great by designing such a place for the Nazis, then I am sure that the donor of the stone would have been elevated, too. Personal power played very heavy parts for the high players during Nazi Germany. I thought to myself that I should like to have seen Germania built, just to see it. I was certainly impressed with the design and how high it was. What was in the back of my mind, looking at it, and everything else about Germany, was wondering how somebody had come to have such power, to do and to think such things as Hitler did, and the long sightedness of it all. It still cannot be understood by any nation why and how it was allowed to come into being, because it took the whole of the world five years to bring Germany to heel. No one could comprehend or explain it, not satisfactorily, even today when the War has been over for sixty seven years. I'm sure that ever since the end of that era, right up to the present there is never a day that passes that somewhere in the newspapers, on the radio, somewhere in the country there hasn't been a Lancaster mentioned, or something about the Second World War. The First World War you don't hear mentioned quite as much and what I'm trying to say is why; when you think of all the books that have been written about it, all the friends that have been made over the world, all the scientific achievements and designs, many came as a result of the Second World War. It has changed the way we can grow more food, for everything seemed to be at a standstill during the two wars, but our technology hasn't stopped evolving since World War II. So thinking to myself about it and analysing it the best that I can, I've come to the conclusion that everything Hitler did, thought and tried to achieve, the end product was evil. I am sure that if it had been for the good, not evil, he would have had Germania built, ninety seven metres to its highest point.

I remember talking to our German historian as our visit was coming to an end and I was saying how wonderful and beautiful I thought Germany was, so much so that I said that I could easily move to Germany to live and he turned to me very seriously and said, "Don't you ever think about coming to live here, Fred. We've got nothing to celebrate, but Britain's got everything to be proud of, " and that really stayed with me. I think that from the whole visit to Berlin, the thing that gave me the most pleasure and made me feel happy and satisfied was the night before we flew back to England. The evening before we left, the German historian who had been with us for the week, invited my accompanying friends and me to go to his house to have a glass of wine and some cake that his wife had kindly made for us, to say 'cheerio'. Our historian friend lived in a very old German house which had not been bombed during the War. When we were sitting together and settled, the five of us all together, having the cake and wine, I was thinking to myself that I never, ever expected, in my life to be sitting in a German house with a German man and his wife, thinking about my brother who had been shot down over Nuremberg and killed. I was wondering what my father and mother would have thought of me if they had been alive. I remember very well that when Chris was killed, Father was devastated and I'm sure that he couldn't speak one good word about the German people, ever. And yet, here we were in the German historian's house, enjoying our wine together, whilst his wife sat happily talking to me and everybody was friends. Over thirty years ago, when I went to Germany for the first time, to find my brother's grave and researched a lot of the history, I came to the conclusion that it was time to forgive. And it has dawned on me, as I get older, if I can't forgive, then how can I expect to be forgiven? So now, *all* is forgiven. Many of those Germans didn't want a war, any more than we did and I know for *sure* that my father, before he died, had forgiven as well. So I was satisfied to think to myself, "Mission accomplished," and I came away very happy that everything has been forgiven.

I have found out in my lifetime, it's a very difficult thing to explain, and I understand that you can say to yourself "I'll never, ever forgive," but the fact is, that if you truly want to be happy in your life, the only way to achieve this is to forgive. To try to accept the frailty and imperfection in human nature just as it is, which means accepting the ignorance and weaknesses of others and ourselves, because this is the only thing which will give you peace.

Durnbach War Memorial

The Pantons and friends at Durnbach War Cemetery

Visiting Chris's final resting place

Chapter Twenty Two

Through Fred's Eyes

After telling you my story and explaining the things that I have accomplished in my life up to this point, I wanted to finish this book by giving you what I have found to be life's secrets. These things have all, I believe, brought me much happiness, success, comfort and love in my lifetime and I believe that they have been fundamental in my achievements. They are what keep me going everyday and they make me feel like I am living my life the way it was supposed to be lived. I hope this can be of some use to you, in some way, in your life too.

I have found that there is no more honourable trait in a person than honesty. Never be frightened of facing the facts, whether they're good or bad, you can squarely face the facts and be honest. I have always, without exception, found that people always respect honesty. I have also found that it has always served me to have respect for every person, no matter who it is that you are speaking to. Your life is only as good as the people who make it and this World can only be as good as you want to make it. You can always get the best from a person, when you give them the same respect as you would expect yourself. After all, we are all the same, however different our lives may appear; we are the same creatures with the same emotions and needs. As a business owner, it's always good practice to give your workers the very best you're capable of giving them, with generosity. As the years go by and you gain more experience, you begin to build a bigger picture of what this life's about and what you're responsible for. As you grow in your business and in your success you should never succumb to changing your personality. It is false to show any boastfulness or cleverness, or to think; "I am the great *I am.*" It is important to always have in the back of your mind that you have done nothing special and what's the next goal? Of course, I do not mean to not be grateful, or to not be proud of your accomplishments, but staying grounded is staying sane. Thoughts should be of equality with every person. Building can be done on the right foundations and that must be in the forefront of your thinking.

Life can throw us many challenges, but never be defeated by obstacles that come in your way. Keep on a straight road until you have achieved your goal. Life always has disappointments, but you can look back on them and see lessons that came from them. Inner strength comes from your beliefs, which keep you strong. As the years go by, if you keep acting on what you want, you're given a certain energy to continue with your life, on your mission, and to do as much as possible in this life. To leave behind something greater than when you first arrived, to leave the World a better place. You want to be able to say that you've left your mark, improved the World just a little more. As long as what you think of and desire is going to be beneficial and valuable to other people, then it's bound to come about for you. It all depends on how far you want to build and progress in life and business, the sky is the limit.

One of the most important things, to me, is my faith. Whatever your beliefs are, if you believe in the greater good and working towards a better outcome then you will always be on the right road. It's up to you how big you want to take it, how high you want to fly, or how small you want to keep it; you decide your life. Tomorrow isn't decided by yesterday, every day is a clean slate. Christianity is my belief and so I live in this way. I find comfort and help in prayer and I have personally found that it is the secret to success. It can be very much the secret power in anybody's life, providing you believe in what you're praying for and who you're praying to. You must always think that who you are addressing is very real. That they hear every word you say and know, beyond your words, how you truly feel. If you do trust with all your heart, then you can be assured that you will be looked after. It will not do anything for you to pray disbelievingly, with fear or doubt. There is no other way, so if you are genuine in what you say, then who you believe in will honour you, if you really are sincere. One of the most important things you must put right on your journey through life, is that you must have the right foundations on which to build your experience of life and this applies to everything. If you build your life based on dishonesty, cheating and selfishness, then that is all you will get back, but if you live in a way that *feels* right, your World will seem a much brighter, safer place.

Of course, if you can do these things then you will naturally have a strong faith in what you're doing, it happens automatically because you know you're being backed up by something greater than yourself, and no one can take it away or stop it! Now, I realise that what I am saying are strong words to many, but my life experience and my feelings ask that I reach out and help anyone who is really listening to the meaning of what I am saying.

I can honestly say that if I had my time over again, I would not change a thing. I would live though all the hard times and all the good times and I would marry the same wonderful girl.

My mission is almost accomplished.

God bless you and yours.

Fred and Harold are presented with a Life-time Achievement Award by Prince Michael of Kent

Fred's parents with some
of their family

Fred & Betty with family and friends at
Lancaster House

Fred & Betty surrounded by visitors on the runway with 'Just Jane'

The opening of the Aviation Heritage Museum

Fred with Queen Mary at the museum

Fred's carriage

Fred with his 'four in hand'

Fred and Harold with Stephen Fry

Harry Secombe with Fred and Harold

Stephen Fry with Betty

The real Just Jane visiting 'Just Jane'

The President, Chairman and Council of The Air League

request the pleasure of the company of

Mr F Panton and Guest

at a Reception to be held at

St James's Palace, London SW1

in the presence of

His Royal Highness The Duke of Edinburgh KG KT

on Wednesday, 4 June 2008

Reception 6.15-8.15 pm

Dress: Lounge Suit

RSVP: The Director, The Air League, Broadway House, Tothill Street, London SW1H 9NS

Invitation from the Council of the Air League

The Duke of Edinburgh with Fred and Harold